THE BOOK

Gospel Songs

T0045634

ISBN 0-634-02017-X

HAL•LEONARD®
CORPORATION
7777 W. BLUEMOUND RD. P.O. BOX 13819 MILWAUKEE, WI 53213

Visit Hal Leonard Online at
www.halleonard.com

THE Gospel Songs BOOK

4	*Strum and Pick Patterns*
5	Amazing Grace
6	Are You Washed in the Blood?
7	At Calvary
8	At the Cross
9	Because He Lives
12	Blessed Assurance
13	Blessed Be the Name
14	The Blood Will Never Lose Its Power
16	Broken and Spilled Out
15	Calvary Covers It All
18	Church in the Wildwood
10	The Day He Wore My Crown
19	Do Lord
20	Does Jesus Care?
21	Down at the Cross (Glory to His Name)
22	The Eastern Gate
23	Footsteps of Jesus
24	Give Me That Old Time Religion
26	God Is So Good
25	God Will Take Care of You
26	Goodby, World, Goodby
28	Hallelujah, We Shall Rise
29	He Keeps Me Singing
30	He Looked Beyond My Fault
31	He Touched Me
32	He's Got the Whole World in His Hands
33	Higher Ground
34	His Eye Is on the Sparrow
35	His Name Is Wonderful
36	How Great Thou Art
37	How Long Has It Been
38	I Am Not Ashamed
40	I Bowed on My Knees and Cried Holy
42	I Have Decided to Follow Jesus
43	I Love to Tell the Story
44	I Saw the Light
45	I Stand Amazed in the Presence (My Savior's Love)
46	I Will Serve Thee
47	I'd Rather Have Jesus
48	I'll Fly Away
49	I'm Standing on the Solid Rock
50	I've Got Peace Like a River
51	In the Garden
52	It Is Well With My Soul
53	Jesus Is the Sweetest Name I Know
41	Jesus Loves the Little Children
54	Jesus Paid It All
55	Joshua (Fit the Battle of Jericho)
56	Just a Closer Walk With Thee
57	Just As I Am
58	The King Is Coming
60	Lamb of Glory
62	Leaning on the Everlasting Arms
63	Let Us Break Bread Together
64	Life's Railway to Heaven
65	The Lighthouse

66	The Lily of the Valley
67	Little Is Much When God Is in It
68	The Longer I Serve Him
69	Love Lifted Me
70	The Love of God
71	Mansion Over the Hilltop
72	Midnight Cry
76	More Than Wonderful
75	My God Is Real (Yes, God Is Real)
78	My Savior First of All
80	My Tribute
79	A New Name in Glory
82	Nothing But the Blood
83	Oh, How I Love Jesus
84	The Old Rugged Cross
85	On Jordan's Stormy Banks
86	(There'll Be) Peace in the Valley (For Me)
87	Precious Lord, Take My Hand (Take My Hand, Precious Lord)
88	Precious Memories
73	Put Your Hand in the Hand
90	Rise Again
92	Rock of Ages
89	Room at the Cross for You
94	Shall We Gather at the River?
95	Since Jesus Came Into My Heart
96	Soon and Very Soon
97	Stepping on the Clouds
98	Sweet Beulah Land
99	Sweet By and By
100	Sweet, Sweet Spirit
92	Tears Are a Language God Understands
101	There Is a Fountain
102	There Is Power in the Blood
103	There's Something About That Name
104	'Tis So Sweet to Trust in Jesus
105	Turn Your Radio On
108	The Unclouded Day
106	Victory in Jesus
109	Wayfaring Stranger
110	We Are So Blessed
111	We Shall Behold Him
114	We'll Understand It Better By and By
115	Were You There?
116	What a Day That Will Be
117	What a Friend We Have in Jesus
118	When I Can Read My Title Clear
119	When the Roll Is Called Up Yonder
120	When We All Get to Heaven
112	Whispering Hope
121	Why Me? (Why Me, Lord?)
124	Will the Circle Be Unbroken
125	Wings of a Dove
126	Without Him
127	The Wonder of It All
122	Wonderful Grace of Jesus
128	Written in Red

STRUM AND PICK PATTERNS

This chart contains the suggested strum and pick patterns that are referred to by number at the beginning
of each song in this book. The symbols ⊓ and ∨ in the strum patterns refer to down and up strokes, respectively.
The letters in the pick patterns indicate which right-hand fingers plays which strings.

p = thumb
i = index finger
m = middle finger
a = ring finger

For example; Pick Pattern 2
is played: thumb - index - middle - ring

Strum Patterns

Pick Patterns

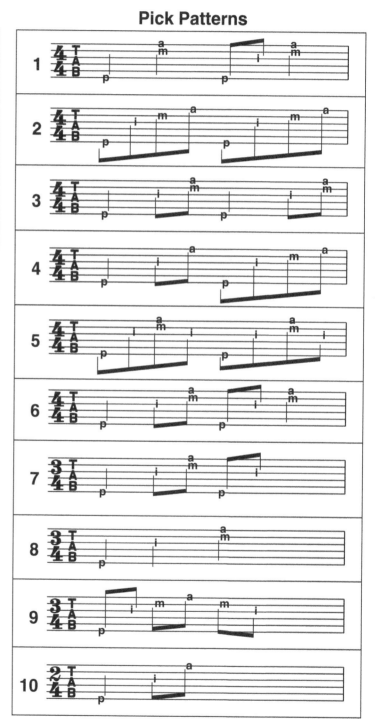

You can use the 3/4 Strum or Pick Patterns in songs written in compound meter (6/8, 9/8, 12/8, etc.).
For example, you can accompany a song in 6/8 by playing the 3/4 pattern twice in each measure.
The 4/4 Strum and Pick Patterns can be used for songs written in cut time (¢) by doubling the note
time values in the patterns. Each pattern would therefore last two measures in cut time.

Amazing Grace

Words by John Newton
Traditional American Melody

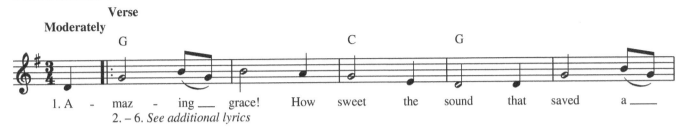

Strum Pattern: 7
Pick Pattern: 7

Verse
Moderately

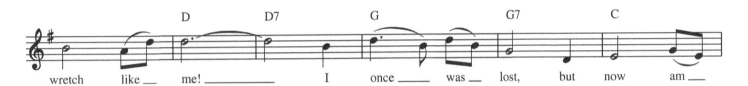

1. A - maz - ing ___ grace! How sweet the sound that saved a ___
2. – 6. *See additional lyrics*

wretch like ___ me! ___ I once ___ was ___ lost, but now am ___

found, was blind, but ___ now I see. ___ 2. 'Twas ___

Additional Lyrics

2. 'Twas grace that taught my heart to fear,
   And grace my fears relieved.
   How precious did that grace appear
   The hour I first believed.

3. Through many dangers, toils and snares,
   I have already come.
   'Tis grace has brought me safe thus far,
   And grace will lead me home.

4. The Lord has promised good to me,
   His word my hope secures.
   He will my shield and portion be
   As long as life endures.

5. And when this flesh and heart shall fail,
   And mortal life shall cease.
   I shall posess within the veil
   A life of joy and peace.

6. When we've been there ten thousand years,
   Bright shining as the sun.
   We've no less days to sing God's praise
   Than when we first begun.

Are You Washed in the Blood?

Words and Music by Elisha A. Hoffman

Strum Pattern: 5
Pick Pattern: 5

1. Have you been to Je-sus for the cleans-ing power? Are you
2., 3., 4. *See additional lyrics*

washed in the blood of the Lamb? Are you ful-ly trust-ing in His

grace this hour? Are you washed in the blood of the Lamb? Are you

Chorus

washed in the blood, in the soul-cleans-ing blood of the Lamb? Are your

gar-ments spot-less? Are they white as snow? Are you washed in the blood of the Lamb? 2. Are you Lamb!

Additional Lyrics

2. Are you walking daily by the Savior's side?
   Are you washed in the blood of the Lamb?
   Do you rest each moment in the Crucified?
   Are you washed in the blood of the Lamb?

3. When the Bridegroom cometh will your robes be white?
   Are you washed in the blood of the Lamb?
   Will your soul be ready for the mansions bright,
   And be washed in the blood of the Lamb?

4. Lay aside the garments that are stained with sin,
   And be washed in the blood of the Lamb.
   There's a fountain flowing for the soul unclean,
   Oh be washed in the blood of the Lamb!

At Calvary

Words by William R. Newell
Music by Daniel B. Towner

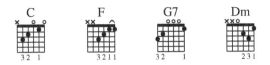

Strum Pattern: 3
Pick Pattern: 3

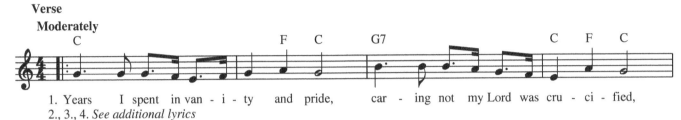

1. Years I spent in van - i - ty and pride, car - ing not my Lord was cru - ci - fied,
2., 3., 4. *See additional lyrics*

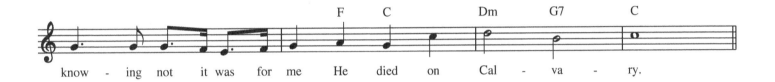

know - ing not it was for me He died on Cal - va - ry.

Chorus

Mer - cy there was great and grace was free, par - don there was mul - ti - plied to me,

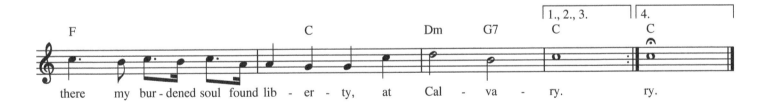

there my bur - dened soul found lib - er - ty, at Cal - va - ry. ry.

Additional Lyrics

2. By God's Word at last my sin I learned,
   Then I trembled at the law I'd spurned,
   Till my guilty soul imploring turned to Calvary.

3. Now I've giv'n to Jesus ev'rything
   Now gladly own Him as my King,
   Now my raptured soul can only sing of Calvary.

4. Oh the love that drew salvation's plan!
   Oh the grace that brought it down to man!
   Oh the mighty gulf that God did span at Calvary.

At the Cross

Words by Isaac Watts and Ralph E. Hudson
Music by Ralph E. Hudson

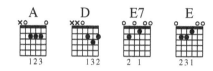

Strum Pattern: 2
Pick Pattern: 4

Verse
Moderately

1. A - las! And did my Sav - ior bleed, and did my Sov - reign
2., 3., 4. *See additional lyrics*

die? Would He de - vote that sa - cred head for sin - ners such as

Chorus

I? At the cross, at the cross where I first ___ saw the light and the

bur - den of my heart rolled a - way, it was there by faith I re -

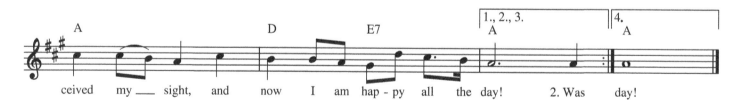

ceived my ___ sight, and now I am hap - py all the day! 2. Was day!

Additional Lyrics

2. Was it for crimes that I have done He groaned upon the tree?
   Amazing pity! Grace unknown! And love beyond degree!

3. Well might the sun in darkness hole and shut His glories in,
   When Christ, the mighty Maker, died for man the creature's sin.

4. But drops of grief can ne'er repay the debt of love I owe:
   Here, Lord, I give myself away; 'tis all that I can do!

Because He Lives

Words by William J. and Gloria Gaither

Music by William J. Gaither

Strum Pattern: 3
Pick Pattern: 3

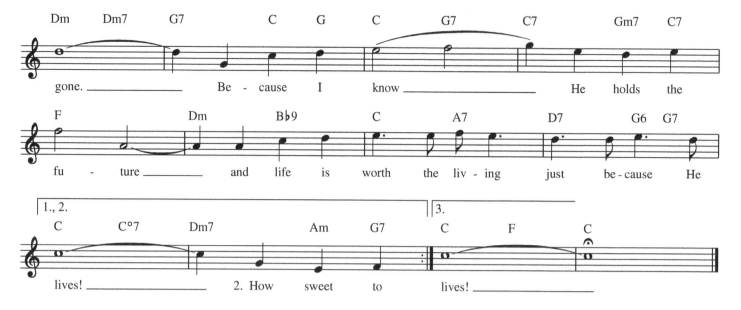

gone. _____ Be - cause I know _____ He holds the

fu - ture _____ and life is worth the liv - ing just be - cause He

lives! _____ 2. How sweet to lives! _____

Additional Lyrics

2. How sweet to hold our newborn baby,
   And feel the pride and joy He gives.
   But greater still the calm assurance,
   This child can face uncertain days because He lives.

3. And then one day I'll cross that river,
   I'll fight life's final war with pain.
   And then as death gives way to vict'ry,
   I'll see the lights of glory and I'll know He reigns.

The Day He Wore My Crown

Words and Music by Phil Johnson

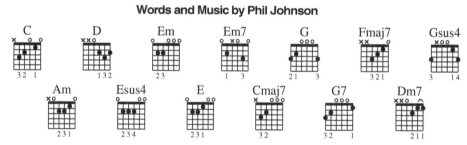

Strum Pattern: 3, 4
Pick Pattern: 1, 3

Verse
Reflectively

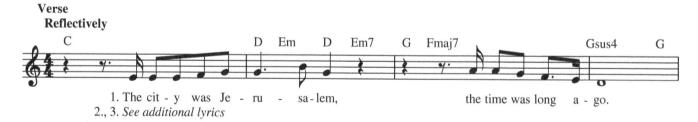

1. The cit - y was Je - ru - sa - lem, the time was long a - go.
2., 3. *See additional lyrics*

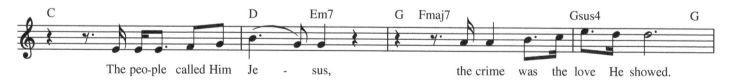

The peo-ple called Him Je - sus, the crime was the love He showed.

Chorus

And I'm the one to blame; I caused all the pain.

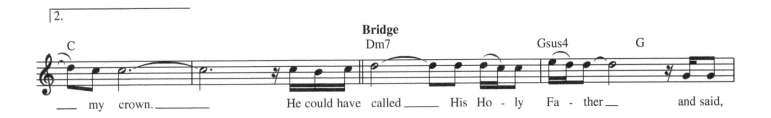

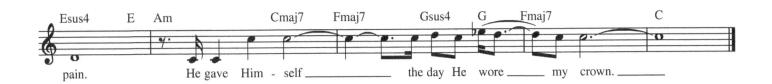

Additional Lyrics

2. He brought me love that only He could give,
   I brought Him cause to cry.
   And though He taught me how to live
   I taught Him how to die.

3. But he walked right through the gate
   And then on up the hill.
   And as He fell beneath the weight,
   He cried, "Father, not my will."

Blessed Assurance

Lyrics by Fanny J. Crosby
Music by Phoebe Palmer Knapp

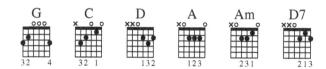

Strum Pattern: 8
Pick Pattern: 8

Verse
Moderately

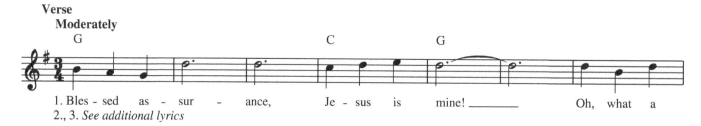

1. Bles - sed as - sur - ance, Je - sus is mine! _____ Oh, what a
2., 3. *See additional lyrics*

fore - taste of glo - ry di - vine! _____ Heir of sal - va - tion,

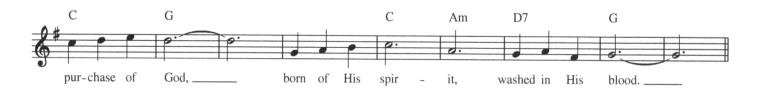

pur - chase of God, _____ born of His spir - it, washed in His blood. _____

Chorus

This is my sto - ry, this is my song, _____ prais - ing my Sav -

ior all the day long. _____ This is my sto - ry, this is my

song, _____ prais - ing my Sav - ior all the day long. _____

Additional Lyrics

2. Perfect submission, perfect delight,
   Visions of rapture now burst on my sight.
   Angels descending, bring from above
   Echoes of mercy, whispers of love.

3. Perfect submission, all is at rest.
   I in my Savior am happy and blest.
   Watching and waiting, looking above,
   Filled with His goodness, lost in His love.

Blessed Be the Name

Words by William H. Clark (verses) and Ralph E. Hudson (refrain)
Traditional
Arranged by Ralph E. Hudson and William J. Kirkpatrick

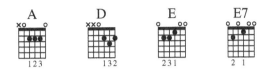

Strum Pattern: 5, 6
Pick Pattern: 4, 5

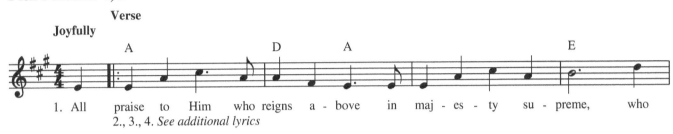

Additional Lyrics

2. His name above all names shall stand,
   Exalted more and more,
   At God the Father's own right hand,
   Where angel hosts adore.

3. Redeemer, Savior, friend of man,
   Once ruined by the fall,
   Thou hast devised salvation's plan,
   For thou hast died for all.

4. His name above all names shall stand,
   Exalted more and more,
   At all earth's kingdoms conqueror,
   Whose reign shall never cease.

The Blood Will Never Lose Its Power

Words and Music by Andraé Crouch

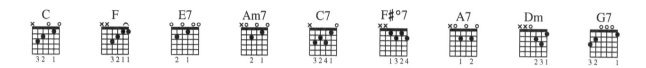

Strum Pattern: 7, 8
Pick Pattern: 7, 8

Verse
Broadly

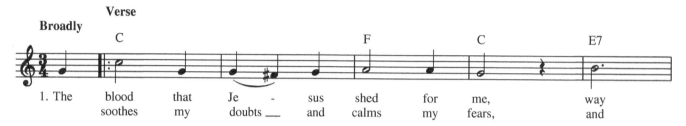

1. The blood that Je - sus shed for me, way
soothes my doubts __ and calms my fears, and

back on Cal - va - ry. The blood that gives me strength from
it dries all my tears.

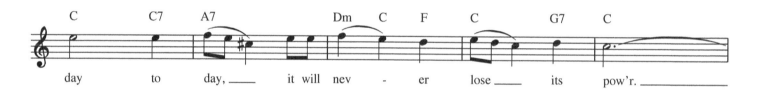

day to day, __ it will nev - er lose __ its pow'r. __

Chorus

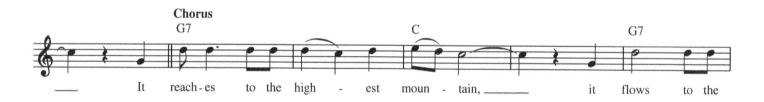

__ It reach - es to the high - est moun - tain, __ it flows to the

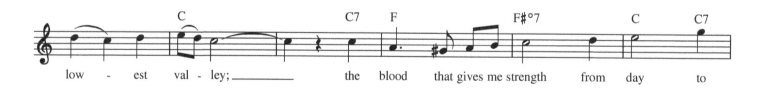

low - est val - ley; __ the blood that gives me strength from day to

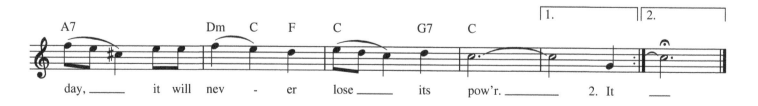

day, __ it will nev - er lose __ its pow'r. __ 2. It __

Calvary Covers It All

Words and Music by Mrs. Walter Taylor

Strum Pattern: 7, 8
Pick Pattern: 7, 8

Additional Lyrics

2. The stripes that He bore and the thorns that He wore
   Told His mercy and love evermore;
   And my heart bowed in shame as I called on His name
   And Calvary covers it all.

Broken and Spilled Out

Words by Gloria Gaither
Music by Bill George

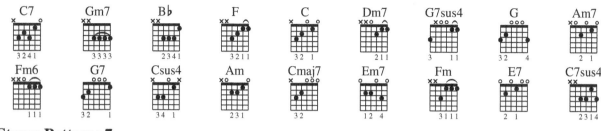

Strum Pattern: 7
Pick Pattern: 8

Chorus

Warmly

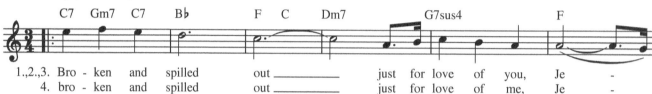

1.,2.,3. Bro - ken and spilled out _____ just for love of you, Je -
4. bro - ken and spilled out _____ just for love of me, Je -

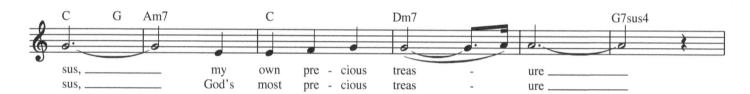

sus, _____ my own pre - cious treas - ure _____
sus, _____ God's most pre - cious treas - ure _____

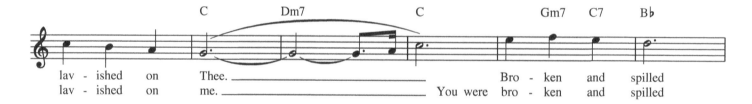

lav - ished on Thee. _____ Bro - ken and spilled
lav - ished on me. _____ You were bro - ken and spilled

out _____ and poured at Your feet; _____
out _____ and poured at my feet; _____

To Coda

in sweet a - ban - don, let me be spilled _ out _____ and used up for
in sweet a - ban - don, Lord, You were spilled _ out _____ and used up for

Verse

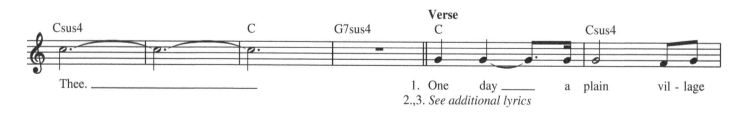

Thee. _____ 1. One day _____ a plain vil - lage
2.,3. *See additional lyrics*

wom - an   driv - en ____ by love   for her Lord, ____

reck - less - ly   poured out ____ a val - ua - ble es - sence, _   dis - re - gard - ing the

scorn. ____   And once   it   was bro - ken   and   spilled _ out,   a

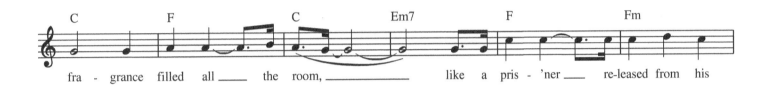

fra - grance   filled   all ____ the room, ____   like   a pris - 'ner ____ re-leased from his

shack - les, ____   like   a spir - it   set   free   from the   tomb.   me!   You were

♦ **Coda**

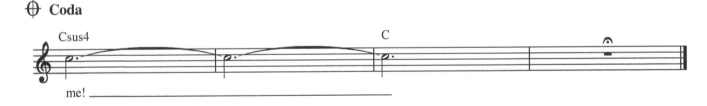

me! ____

Additional Lyrics

2. Whatever it takes to be Yours, Lord,
   Whatever it takes to be clean,
   I just can't live without Your sweet approval,
   No matter what it may mean!
   I throw myself at Your feet, Lord,
   Broken by Your love for me;
   May the fragrance of total commitment
   Be the only defense that I need.

3. Lord, You were God's precious treasure,
   His loved and His own perfect Son,
   Sent here to show me the love of the Father;
   Yes, just for love it was done!
   And though You were perfect and holy,
   You gave up Yourself willingly;
   And You spared no expense for my pardon,
   You were spilled out and wasted for me!

The Church in the Wildwood

Words and Music by Dr. William S. Pitts

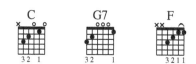

Strum Pattern: 3, 4
Pick Pattern: 1, 3

Moderately

Verse

1. There's a church in the val-ley by the wild - wood, no love - li - er spot in the
2., 3. *See additional lyrics*

dale; no _____ place is so dear to my child - hood as the

Chorus

lit - tle brown church in the vale. Oh, _____ come, come, come, come, come to the church in the

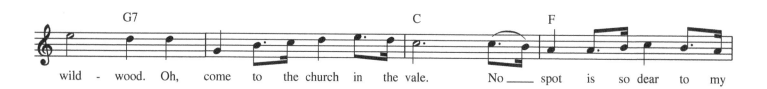

wild - wood. Oh, come to the church in the vale. No _____ spot is so dear to my

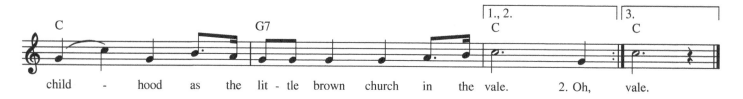

child - hood as the lit - tle brown church in the vale. 2. Oh, vale.

Additional Lyrics

2. Oh, come to the church in the wildwood,
   To the trees where the wild flowers bloom;
   Where the parting hymn will be chanted
   We will weep by the side of the tomb.

3. From the church in the valley by the wildwood,
   When day fades away into night;
   I would fain from this spot of my childhood
   Wing my way to the mansions of light.

Do Lord

Traditional

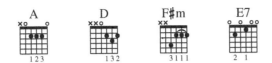

Strum Pattern: 1, 3
Pick Pattern: 2, 4

Verse
Joyfully

1. I've got a home in glo-ry land that out-shines the sun. I've got a home in glo-ry land that
2. *See additional lyrics*

out-shines the sun. I've got a home in glo-ry land that out-shines the sun,

Chorus

way be-yond _ the blue. Do Lord, oh do Lord, oh do re-mem-ber me.

Do Lord, oh do Lord, oh do re-mem-ber me. Do Lord, oh do Lord, oh

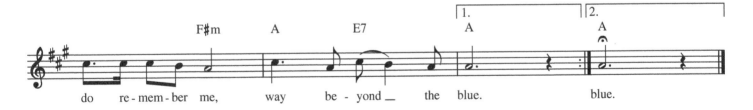

do re-mem-ber me, way be-yond _ the blue. blue.

Additional Lyrics

2. I took Jesus as my Saviour, you take Him too.
I took Jesus as my Saviour, you take Him too.
I took Jesus as my Saviour, you take Him too.
While He's calling you.

Does Jesus Care?

Words by Frank E. Graeff
Music by J. Lincoln Hall

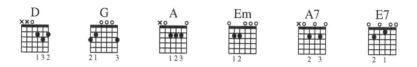

Strum Pattern: 7, 8
Pick Pattern: 7, 8

Verse
Moderately

1. Does Je - sus care when my heart is pained too deep - ly for mirth and song, ___ as the
2., 3., 4. *See additional lyrics*

bur - dens press, and the cares dis - tress, and the way grows wea - ry and long? ___ Oh

Chorus

yes, He cares, I know He cares; His heart is touched with my grief. ___ When the

days are wea - ry, the long nights drear - y, I know my Sav - ior cares. ___ 2. Does cares. ___

Additional Lyrics

2. Does Jesus care when my way is dark
   With a nameless dread and fear?
   As the daylight fades into deep nightshades
   Does he care enough to be near?

3. Does Jesus care when I've tried and failed
   To resist temptation strong,
   When for my deep grief I find no relief
   Though my tears flow all the night long?

4. Does Jesus care when I've said goodbye
   To the dearest on earth to me,
   And my sad heart aches till it nearly breaks
   Is it aught to Him? Does he see?

Down at the Cross
(Glory to His Name)

Words by Elisha A. Hoffman
Music by John H. Stockton

Strum Pattern: 3, 4
Pick Pattern: 1, 3

Additional Lyrics

2. I am so wond'rously saved from sin,
   Jesus so sweetly abides within,
   There at the cross where He took me in.
   Glory to His name!

3. O precious fountain that saves from sin,
   I am so glad that I entered in,
   There Jesus saves me and keeps me clean.
   Glory to His name!

4. Come to this fountain so rich and sweet,
   Cast thy poor soul at the Savior's feet,
   Plunge in today and be made complete.
   Glory to His name!

The Eastern Gate

Words and Music by Isaiah G. Martin

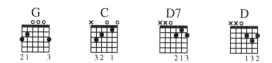

Strum Pattern: 1, 3
Pick Pattern: 2, 4

Verse
Moderately

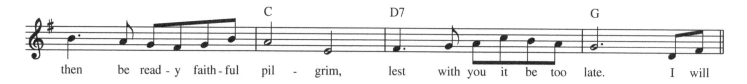

1. I will meet you in the morn - ing, just in - side the East - ern Gate;
2.,3.,4. *See additional lyrics*

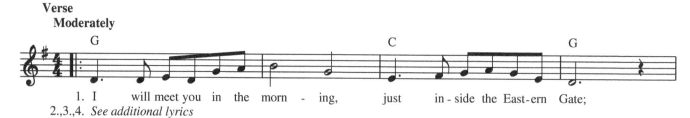

then be read - y faith - ful pil - grim, lest with you it be too late. I will

Chorus

meet you in the morn - ing, I will meet you in the morn - ing, just in - side the East - ern Gate o - ver

there. I will meet you in the morn - ing, I will meet you in the morn - ing, I will

meet you in the morn - ing o - ver there. there.

Additional Lyrics

2. If you hasten off to glory
   Linger near the Eastern Gate;
   For I'm coming in the morning,
   So you'll not have long to wait.

3. Keep your lamps all trimmed and burning,
   For the Bridegroom watch and wait.
   He'll be with us at the meeting,
   Just inside the Eastern Gate!

4. O, the joy of that glad meeting
   With the saints who for us wait!
   What a blessed happy meeting,
   Just inside the Eastern Gate!

Footsteps of Jesus

Words by Mary B.C. Slade
Music by Asa B. Everett

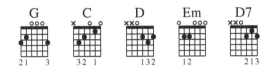

Strum Pattern: 2, 4
Pick Pattern: 1, 3

Verse
Moderately slow

1. Sweet - ly, Lord, have we heard Thee call - ing, "Come, fol - low Me!"
2., 3., 4. *See additional lyrics*

And we see where Thy foot - prints fall - ing, lead us to Thee.

Chorus

Foot - prints of Je - sus that make the path - way glow;

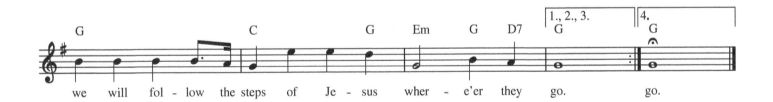

we will fol - low the steps of Je - sus wher - e'er they go. go.

Additional Lyrics

2. Though they lead o'er the cold, dark mountains, seeking His sheep,
   Or along by Siloam's fountains, helping the weak.

3. If they lead through the temple holy, preaching the Word,
   Or in homes of the poor and lowly, serving the Lord.

4. Then at last, when on high he sees us, our journey done,
   We will rest where the steps of Jesus end at His throne.

Give Me That Old Time Religion

Traditional

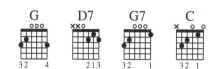

Strum Pattern: 3
Pick Pattern: 2, 5

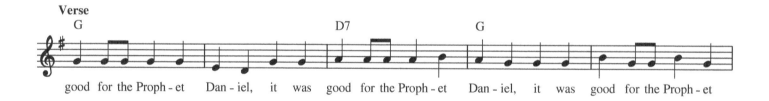

Additional Lyrics

2. It was good for Paul and Silas,
   It was good for Paul and Silas,
   It was good for Paul and Silas,
   And it's good enough for me.

3. It was good for old Abe Lincoln,
   It was good for old Abe Lincoln,
   It was good for old Abe Lincoln,
   And it's good enough for me.

God Will Take Care of You

Words by Civilla D. Martin
Music by W. Stillman Martin

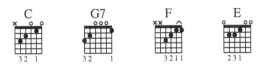

Strum Pattern: 7, 8
Pick Pattern: 7, 8

Verse
Moderately

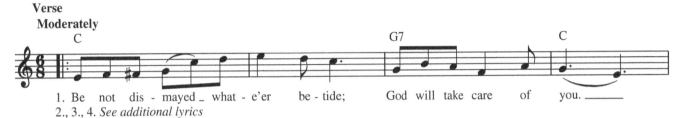

1. Be not dis-mayed _ what-e'er be-tide; God will take care of you. _
2., 3., 4. *See additional lyrics*

Be-neath His wings _ of love a-bide; God will take care of you.

Chorus

God will take care of you, through ev-'ry day, o'er all the way.

He will take care _ of you; God will take care _ of you. you.

Additional Lyrics

2. Through days of toil when heart doth fail,
   God will take care of you.
   When dangers fierce your path assail,
   God will take care of you.

3. All you may need He will provide;
   God will take care of you.
   Nothing you ask will be denied;
   God will take care of you.

4. No matter what may be the test,
   God will take care of you.
   Lean, weary one, upon His breast,
   God will take care of you.

God Is So Good

Traditional

Strum Pattern: 2, 4
Pick Pattern: 4, 5

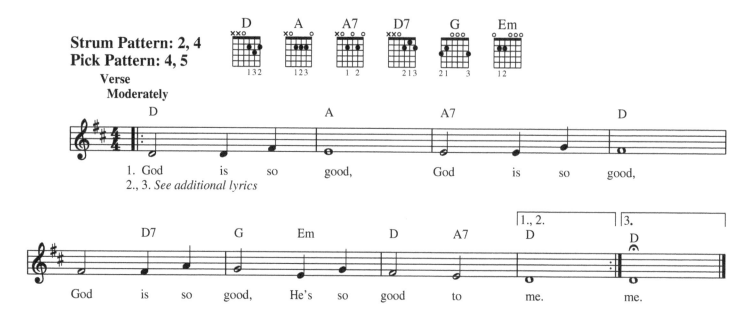

Verse
Moderately

1. God is so good, God is so good,
2., 3. *See additional lyrics*

God is so good, He's so good to me. me.

Additional Lyrics

2. He cares for me, He cares for me,
   He cares for me, He's so good to me.

3. He loves me so, He loves me so,
   He loves me so, He's so good to me.

Goodby, World, Goodby

Words and Music by Mosie Lister

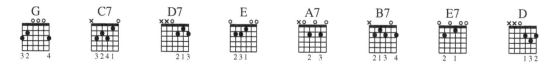

Strum Pattern: 3, 4
Pick Pattern: 1, 3

Lively Verse

1. I've told all my trou-bles good-bye, good-bye to each tear and each sigh; this
2. *See additional lyrics*

world where I roam can-not be my home I'm bound for a land in the sky. I

walk and I talk with my Lord, I feast ev-'ry day on His word.

Heav-en is near, and I can't stay here. Good-bye world, good-bye.____ Now don't you

Chorus

weep for me when I'm gone 'cause I won't have to leave here a-lone. And

when I hear the last trum-pet sound, my feet won't stay on the ground. Gon-na

rise with a shout; gon-na fly,____ gon-na ride with my Lord thru the sky.____

Heav-en is near, and I can't stay here. Good-bye world, good-bye. 2. I bye.

Additional Lyrics

2. I won't have the blues anymore
   When I step across to that shore
   And I'll never pine for I'll leave behind
   My heartaches and tears evermore.
   A day maybe two, then goodbye;
   Tomorrow I'll rise up and fly.
   Heaven is near, and I can't stay here.
   Goodbye world, goodbye.

Hallelujah, We Shall Rise

By J.E. Thomas

Strum Pattern: 1, 2
Pick Pattern: 3, 4

Verse
Joyfully

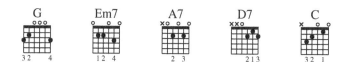

1. In the res-ur-rec-tion morn-ing, when the trump of God shall sound, we shall rise, (Hal-le-lu-jah!) we shall
2., 3., 4. *See additional lyrics*

rise. Then the saints will come re-joic-ing and no tears will e'er be found. We shall

rise, (Hal-le-lu-jah!) in the morn-ing, we shall rise. We shall rise, (Hal-le-lu-jah!) We shall rise. (A-men.) We shall

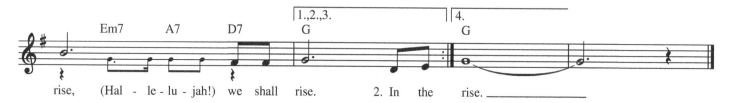

rise. (Hal-le-lu-jah!) In the res-ur-rec-tion morn-ing when death's pris-on bars are bro-ken, we shall

rise, (Hal-le-lu-jah!) we shall rise. 2. In the rise. _____

Additional Lyrics

2. In the resurection morning, what a meeting it will be!
   We shall rise, hallelujah! We shall rise.
   When our fathers and our mothers and our loved ones we shall see!
   We shall rise, hallelujah! In the morning, we shall rise.

3. In the resurrection morning, blessed thought it is to me;
   We shall rise, hallelujah! We shall rise.
   I shall see my blessed Savior, who so freely died for me.
   We shall rise, hallelujah! In the morning, we shall rise.

4. In the resurrection morning, we shall meet Him in the air.
   We shall rise, hallelujah! We shall rise.
   And be carried up to glory, to our home so bright and fair.
   We shall rise, hallelujah! In the morning, we shall rise.

He Keeps Me Singing

Words and Music by Luther B. Bridgers

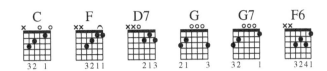

Strum Pattern: 2, 3
Pick Pattern: 3, 4

Verse
Moderately slow

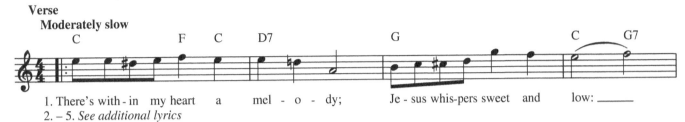

1. There's with-in my heart a mel - o - dy; Je - sus whis-pers sweet and low: _____
2. – 5. *See additional lyrics*

"Fear not, I am with thee; peace, be still," In all of life's ebb and flow.

Chorus

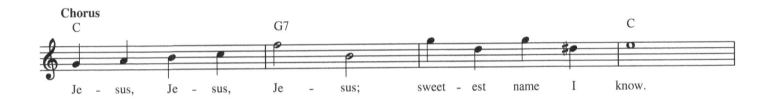

Je - sus, Je - sus, Je - sus; sweet - est name I know.

Fills my ev - 'ry long - ing, keeps me sing-ing as I go. go.

Additional Lyrics

2. All my life was wrecked by sin and strife;
Discord filled my heart with pain.
Jesus swept across the broken strings,
Stirred the slumb'ring chords again.

3. Feasting on the riches of His grace,
Resting 'neath his shelt'ring wing,
Always looking on His smiling face;
That is why I shout and sing:

4. Though sometimes He leads through waters deep,
Trials fall across the way.
Though sometimes the path seems rough and steep,
See His footprints all the way.

5. Soon He's coming back to welcome me
Far beyond the starry sky.
I shall wing my flight to worlds unknown;
I shall reign with Him on high.

He Looked Beyond My Fault

Words and Music by Dottie Rambo

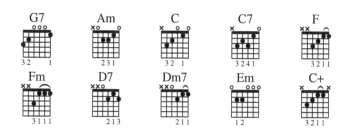

Strum Pattern: 3, 4
Pick Pattern: 1, 3

He Touched Me

Words and Music by William J. Gaither

Strum Pattern: 7, 8
Pick Pattern: 7, 8

Verse
Moderately

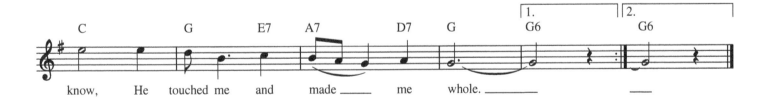

1. Shack - led by a heav - y bur - den _____ 'neath a load of guilt and
2. *See additional lyrics*

shame. _____ Then the hand of Je - sus touched me _____ and now I am no

Chorus

long - er the same. _____ He touched me, ___ oh, He touched me _____ and

oh, the joy that floods my soul. _____ Some-thing ___ hap - pened ___ and now I

know, He touched me and made _____ me whole. _____ ___

Additional Lyrics

2. Since I met this blessed Savior,
   Since He cleansed and me whole,
   I will never cease to praise Him;
   I'll shout it while eternity rolls.

He's Got the Whole World in His Hands

Traditional Spiritual

Strum Pattern: 3, 4
Pick Pattern: 1, 3

1. He's got the whole world __ in His hands, __ He's got the whole world __
   2., 3., 4. *See additional lyrics*

in His hands, __ He's got the whole world __ in His hands, __ He's got the

whole world in His hands. ____ 2. He's got the ____

Additional Lyrics

2. He's got the wind and the rain in His hands,
   He's got the wind and the rain in His hands,
   He's got the wind and the rain in His hands,
   He's got the whole world in His hands.

3. He's got the tiny little baby in His hands,
   He's got the tiny little baby in His hands,
   He's got the tiny little baby in His hands,
   He's got the whole world in His hands.

4. He's got you and me, brother, in His hands,
   He's got you and me, sister, in His hands,
   He's got you and me, brother, in His hands,
   He's got the whole world in His hands.

Higher Ground

Words by Johnson Oatman, Jr.
Music by Charles H. Gabriel

Strum Pattern: 8
Pick Pattern: 8

1. I'm press - ing on the up - ward way, new heights I'm gain - ing ev - 'ry
2., 3., 4. *See additional lyrics*

day; still pray - ing as I'm on-ward bound, "Lord, plant my feet on high - er ground." Lord, lift me

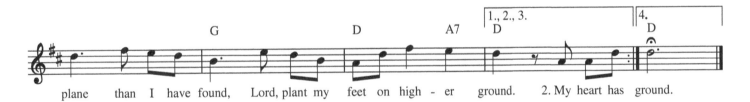

up and let me stand by faith on heav - en's ta - ble - land; a high - er

plane than I have found, Lord, plant my feet on high - er ground. 2. My heart has ground.

Additional Lyrics

2. My heart has no desire to stay
   Where doubts arise and fears dismay;
   Though some may dwell where these abound,
   My prayer, my aim, is higher ground.

3. I want to live above the world,
   Though Satan's darts at me are hurled;
   For faith has caught the joyful sound,
   The song of saints on higher ground.

4. I want to scale the utmost height
   And catch a gleam of glory bright;
   But still I'll pray till heav'n I've found,
   "Lord, lead me on to higher ground."

His Eye Is on the Sparrow

Words by Civilla D. Martin

Music by Charles H. Gabriel

Strum Pattern: 7, 8
Pick Pattern: 7, 8

Additional Lyrics

2. "Let not your heart be troubled," His tender word I hear,
   And resting on His goodness, I lose my doubts and fears.
   Though by the path He leadeth, but one step I may see.
   His eye is on the sparrow and I know He watches me.

3. Whenever I am tempted, whenever clouds arise,
   When song gives place to sighing, when hope within me dies,
   I draw the closer to Him, from care He sets me free.
   His eye is on the sparrow and I know He cares for me.

His Name Is Wonderful

Words and Music by Audrey Mieir

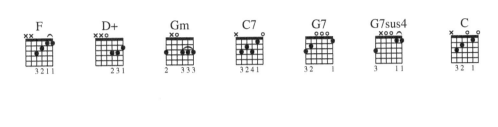

Strum Pattern: 7, 8
Pick Pattern: 7, 8

Verse
Prayerfully

His name __ is Won-der-ful, His name __ is Won-der-ful, His name __ is

Won - der-ful, Je - sus, my Lord. He is _____ the might - y King,

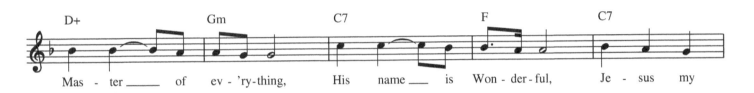

Mas - ter _____ of ev - 'ry-thing, His name __ is Won - der-ful, Je - sus my

Lord. He's the great shep - herd, ___ the Rock of all a - ges,

Al - might - y God is He; _____ bow down __ be - fore Him,

love and ___ a - dore Him, His name __ is Won - der-ful, Je - sus my Lord.

How Great Thou Art

Words and Music by Stuart K. Hine

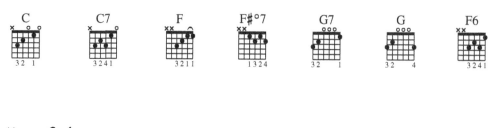

Strum Pattern: 3, 4
Pick Pattern: 1, 3

Majestically

Verse

1. O Lord my God! When I in awe-some won - der ___ con-sid - er all the works Thy hands have
2. *See additional lyrics*

made. I see the stars. I hear the might - y thun - der, ___ Thy pow'r through -

Chorus

out the u - ni-verse dis-played. Then sings my soul, my Sav-ior God to Thee; how great Thou

art! How great Thou art! Then sings my soul, my Sav - ior God to

1.

2.

Thee; how great Thou art! How great Thou art! ___ 2. When Christ shall art!

Additional Lyrics

2. When Christ shall come with shout of acclamation
   And take my home, what joy shall fill my heart!
   Then I shall bow in humble adoration
   And there proclaim, my God, how great Thou art!

How Long Has It Been

Words and Music by Mosie Lister

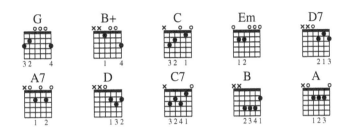

Strum Pattern: 7, 8
Pick Pattern: 7, 8

Additional Lyrics

2. How long has it been since you knelt by your bed,
   And prayed to the Lord up in Heaven?
   How long since you knew that He'd answer you,
   And would keep you the long night through?
   How long has it been since you woke with the dawn,
   And felt that the day's worth the living?
   Can you call Him your Friend?
   How long has it been since you knew that He cared for you?

I Am Not Ashamed

Words and Music by Constant Change

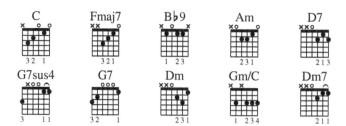

Strum Pattern: 1
Pick Pattern: 2

Verse
Moderately

1. We're an an-chor for those _ who are hurt-ing, ___ we're a har-bor for those _ who are lost.

Some-times it's not _ al - ways eas - y bear-ing Cal - va-ry's cross. ___ We've been

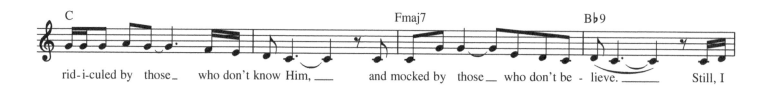

rid-i-culed by those_ who don't know Him, ___ and mocked by those _ who don't be - lieve. ___ Still, I

love stand-ing up for my Je - sus 'cause of all that He's done_ for me. That's why

Chorus

I am not a - shamed _ of the gos - pel, ___ the gos - pel of Je - sus Christ. _ No,

I am not a-fraid _ to be count-ed; ___ I'm will-ing to give _ my life. ___ Now I'm read -

- y to be __ all He wants __ me to be, _____ give up the wrong for the right. ___ Oh no,

To Coda ⊕

I am not a-shamed of the gos - pel, _____ I am not __ a - shamed of the gos - pel of Je - sus

Verse

Christ. _____ 2. For ev-'ry mo-ment His hand __ has had mer - cy, _____ for all the

love He's shown all my life, a sim-ple "thanks" does-n't say how I'm feel - in; I get

tears _ in my eyes. _____ So as for me, __ I'm gon-na keep on be - liev - in' _____ in the

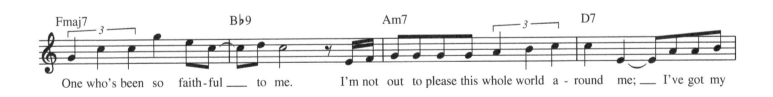

One who's been so faith-ful ___ to me. I'm not out to please this whole world a - round me; ___ I've got my

D.S. al Coda   ⊕ **Coda**

mind on e - ter - ni - ty. That's why   Christ. _____

39

I Bowed on My Knees and Cried Holy

Words by Nettie Dudley Washington
Music by E.M. Dudley Cantwell

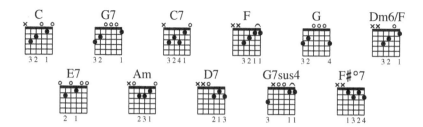

Strum Pattern: 8
Pick Pattern: 8

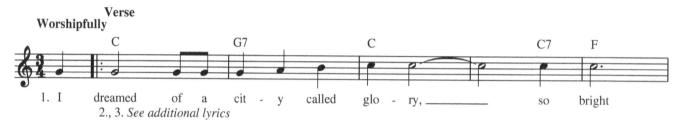

1. I dreamed of a cit - y called glo - ry, _____ so bright

2., 3. *See additional lyrics*

and _____ so fair. _____ When I en - tered the gate I cried,

"Ho - ly," _____ the an - gels all met _____ me there. _____ They

showed me from man - sion to man - sion, _____ and O, the sights _____ I

saw. _____ But I said, "I want to see Je - sus, the _____

One _____ who died _____ for all. _____ Then I bowed on my knees and cried,

"Ho - ly, _____ ho - ly, _____ ho -
ly." I clapped my hands and sang, "Glo - ry, _____
glo - ry to the Son of God." _____ 2. I God." _____

1., 2. | **3.**

Additional Lyrics

2. I thought when I entered that city,
   My friends knew me well.
   They showed me all through Heaven;
   The scenes are too num'rous to tell.
   They showed me Abraham, Isaac, Jacob,
   Mark, Luke, and Timothy.
   But I said, "I want to give praise
   To the One who died for me."

3. I thought when I saw my Saviour,
   O glory to God!
   I just fell right down before Him,
   Singing, "Praise to the name of the Lord."
   I bowed down and worshipped Jehovah,
   My friend of Calvary,
   For I wanted to give praise to Jesus
   For saving a sinner like me.

Jesus Loves the Little Children

Words by Rev. C. H. Woolston
Music by George F. Root

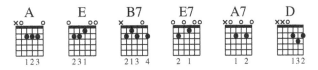

Strum Pattern: 5, 3
Pick Pattern: 4, 5

Happily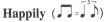

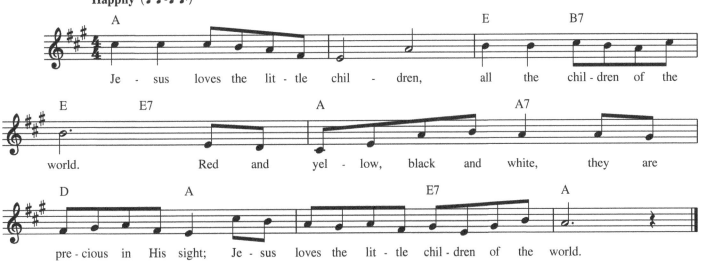

Je - sus loves the lit - tle chil - dren, all the chil - dren of the
world. Red and yel - low, black and white, they are
pre - cious in His sight; Je - sus loves the lit - tle chil - dren of the world.

I Have Decided to Follow Jesus

Folk Melody from India
Arranged by Auila Read

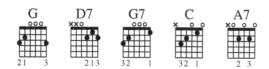

Strum Pattern: 6
Pick Pattern: 4

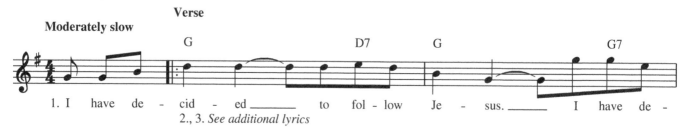

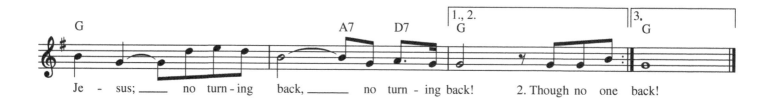

Additional Lyrics

2. Though no one join me, still I will follow.
Though no one join me, still I will follow.
Though no one join me, still I will follow;
No turning back, no turning back!

3. The world behind me, the cross before me;
The world behind me, the cross before me;
The world behind me, the cross before me;
No turning back, no turning back!

I Love to Tell the Story

Words by Catherine Hankey
Music by William G. Fischer

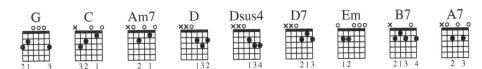

Strum Pattern: 4
Pick Pattern: 4

Verse
Moderately

1. I love to tell the sto - ry of un - seen things _ a - bove, of
2., 3., 4. *See additional lyrics*

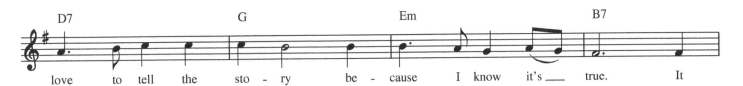

Je - sus and His glo - ry, of ___ Je - sus and ___ His love. I

love to tell the sto - ry be - cause I know it's ___ true. It

sat - is - fies my long - ings as noth - ing else can do. I

Chorus

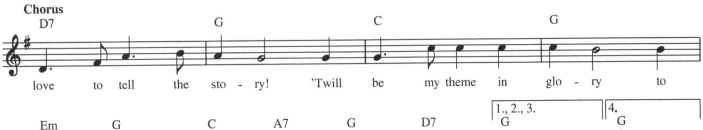

love to tell the sto - ry! 'Twill be my theme in glo - ry to

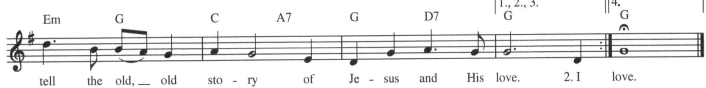

tell the old, _ old sto - ry of Je - sus and His love. 2. I love.

Additional Lyrics

2. I love to tell the story; more wonderful it seems
   Than all the golden fancies of all our golden dreams.
   I love to tell the story; it did so much for me,
   And that is just the reason I tell it now to thee.

3. I love to tell the story; 'tis pleasant to repeat
   What seems each time I tell it, more wonderfully sweet.
   I love to tell the story, for some have never heard
   The message of salvation from God's own holy word.

4. I love to tell the story; for those who know it best
   Seem hungering and thirsting to hear it like the rest.
   And when, in scenes of glory, I sing the new, new song,
   'Twill be the old, old story that I have loved so long.

I Saw the Light

Words and Music by Hank Williams

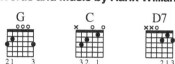

Strum Pattern: 1, 3
Pick Pattern: 2, 4

Lively

Verse

G

1. I wan - dered so aim - less, life filled with sin.

2., 3. *See additional lyrics*

C · · · · · · · · · · · · G

I would - n't let my dear Sav - ior in.

Then Je - sus came like a strang - er in the night.

D7 · · · · · · · · · · G

Praise the Lord, _____ I saw the light.

Chorus

G

I saw the light, _____ I saw the light, _____

C · · · · · · · · · · G

no more in dark - ness, no more in night. _____

Now I'm so hap - py, no sor - row in sight. _____

G · · · D7 · · · | 1., 2. G · · | 3. G

Praise the Lord, _____ I saw the light. light.

Additional Lyrics

2. Just like a blind man I wandered along,
   Worries and fears I claimed for my own.
   Then like the blind man
   That God gave back his sight.

3. I was a fool to wander and stray,
   Straight is the gate and narrow is the way.
   Now I have traded the wrong for the right.
   Praise the Lord, I saw the light.

I Stand Amazed in the Presence
(My Savior's Love)

Words and Music by Charles H. Gabriel

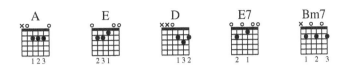

Strum Pattern: 4
Pick Pattern: 3

Verse
Moderately

1. I stand a-mazed in the pres-ence of Je-sus the Naz-a-rene, and

2.-5. *See additional lyrics*

won - der how He could love me, a sin - ner, con - demned, un - clean.

Chorus

How mar - vel-ous! How won - der-ful! And my song shall ev - er be:

How mar - vel-ous! How won - der-ful is my __ Sav - ior's love for me! 2. For love for me!

Additional Lyrics

2. For me it was in the garden He prayed,
   "Not my will, but Thine."
   He had no tears for His own griefs
   But sweat drops of blood for mine.

3. In pity angels beheld Him
   And came from the world of light
   To comfort Him in the sorrows
   He bore before my soul that night.

4. He took my sins and my sorrows,
   He made them His very own.
   He bore the burden to Calv'ry,
   And suffered and died alone.

5. When with the ransomed in glory
   His face I at least shall see,
   'Twill be my joy through the ages
   To sing of His love for me.

I Will Serve Thee

Words by William J. and Gloria Gaither
Music by William J. Gaither

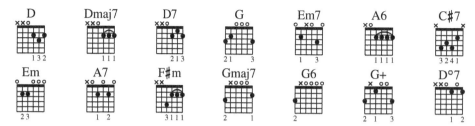

Strum Pattern: 3, 4
Pick Pattern: 1, 3

I'd Rather Have Jesus

Words by Rhea F. Miller

Music by George Beverly Shea

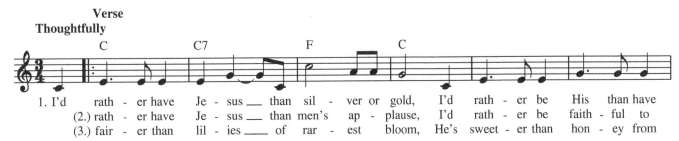

Strum Pattern: 7, 8
Pick Pattern: 7, 8

Verse
Thoughtfully

1. I'd rath - er have Je - sus ___ than sil - ver or gold, I'd rath - er be His than have
(2.) rath - er have Je - sus ___ than men's ap - plause, I'd rath - er be faith - ful to
(3.) fair - er than lil - ies ___ of rar - est bloom, He's sweet - er than hon - ey from

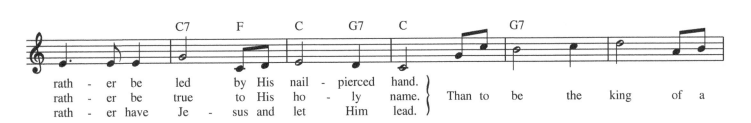

rich - es un - told, I'd rath - er have Je - sus ___ than hous - es or lands. I'd
His ___ dear cause, I'd rath - er have Je - sus ___ than world - wide fame. I'd
out ___ the comb, He's all that my hun - ger - ing spir - it needs. I'd

rath - er be led by His nail - pierced hand. } Than to be the king of a
rath - er be true to His ho - ly name. }
rath - er have Je - sus and let Him lead. }

vast do - main and be held in sin's dread sway. ___ I'd rath - er have Je - sus ___ than

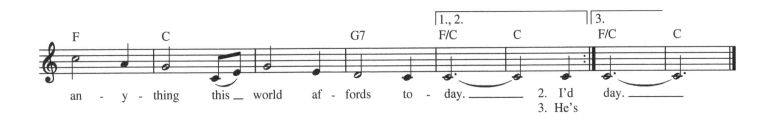

an - y - thing this world af - fords to - day. ___ 2. I'd day. ___
3. He's

I'll Fly Away

Words and Music by Albert E. Brumley

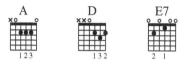

Strum Pattern: 3, 4
Pick Pattern: 1, 3

Verse
Fast

1. Some glad morn-ing when this life is o'er. I'll fly a-way;
2., 3. *See additional lyrics*

to a home on God's ce-les-tial shore. I'll fly a-way.

Chorus

I'll fly a-way, O glo-ry, I'll fly a-way;

when I die Hal-le-lu-jah, by and by, I'll fly a-way. way.

Additional Lyrics

2. Just a few more weary days and then,
   I'll fly away;
   To a land where joys shall never end,
   I'll fly away.

3. When the shadows of this life have grown,
   I'll fly away;
   Like a bird from prison bars have flown,
   I'll fly away.

I'm Standing on the Solid Rock

Words and Music by Harold Lane

Strum Pattern: 3, 4
Pick Pattern: 1, 3

Verse
Joyfully

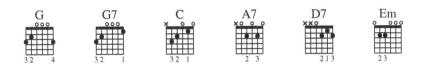

1. Through my dis - ap - point-ments, strife and dis - con - tent-ment, I cast my ev - 'ry care on the
2., 3. *See additional lyrics*

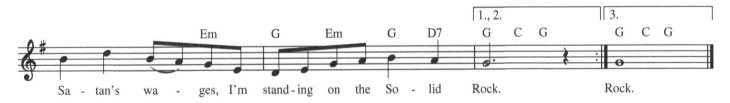

Lord; _____ no mat - ter what ob - ses - sion, pain or deep de - pres - sion, I'm

Chorus

stand-ing on the So - lid Rock. I'm stand - ing on the Rock of A - ges,

safe _____ from all the storm that ra - ges, rich _____ but not from

Sa - tan's wa - ges, I'm stand-ing on the So - lid Rock. Rock.

Additional Lyrics

2. Even though He's gone now, I don't feel alone now,
   With comfort came the Spirit of the Lord;
   Now with His word to guide me, from temptations hide me,
   I'm standing on the Solid Rock.

3. Now, I'm pressing onward, each step leads me homeward,
   I'm trusting in my Savior day by day;
   And close is our relation, firm is it's foundation,
   So on this Solid Rock I'll stay.

I've Got Peace Like a River

Traditional

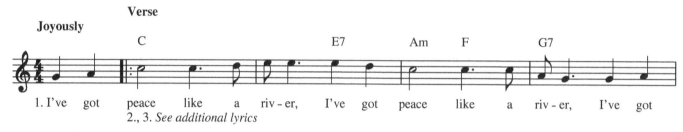

Strum Pattern: 3
Pick Pattern: 3

Verse
Joyously

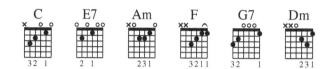

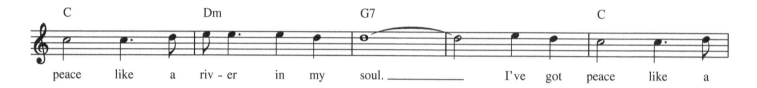

1. I've got peace like a riv - er, I've got peace like a riv - er, I've got
2., 3. *See additional lyrics*

peace like a riv - er in my soul. _____ I've got peace like a

riv - er, I've got peace like a riv - er, I've got peace like a

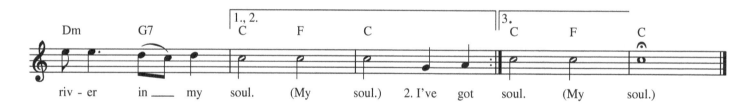

riv - er in __ my soul. (My soul.) 2. I've got soul. (My soul.)

Additional Lyrics

2. I've got love like an ocean,
   I've got love like an ocean,
   I've got love like an ocean in my soul.
   I've got love like an ocean,
   I've got love like an ocean,
   I've got love like an ocean in my soul. (My soul.)

3. I've got joy like a fountain,
   I've got joy like a fountain,
   I've got joy like a fountain in my soul.
   I've got joy like a fountain,
   I've got joy like a fountain,
   I've got joy like a fountain in my soul. (My soul.)

In the Garden

Words and Music by C. Austin Miles

Strum Pattern: 8, 9
Pick Pattern: 8, 9

Verse
Moderately

1. I come to the gar - den a - lone, _____ while the
2., 3. *See additional lyrics*

dew is still on the ros - es, and the voice I hear fall - ing

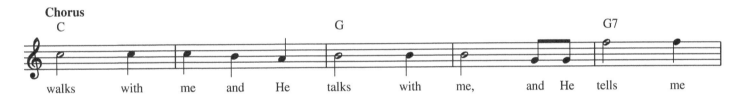

on my ear, the Son of God dis - clos - es, and He

Chorus

walks with me and He talks with me, and He tells me

I am His own, _____ and the joy we share as we tar - ry

there, none oth - er has ev - er known. _____ 2. He

Additional Lyrics

2. He speaks, and the sound of His voice
   Is so sweet the birds hush their singing,
   And the melody that He gave to me
   Within my heart is ringing.

3. I'd stay in the garden with Him,
   Though the night around me be falling.
   But He bids me go through the voice of woe;
   His voice to me is calling.

It Is Well With My Soul

Words by Horatio G. Spafford
Music by Philip P. Bliss

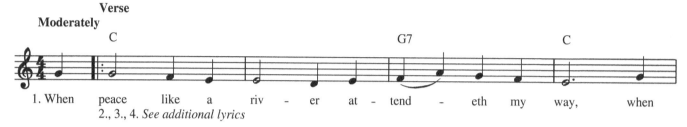

Strum Pattern: 2
Pick Pattern: 2

Verse
Moderately

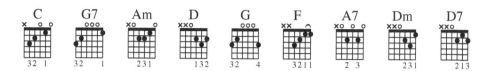

Additional Lyrics

2. Though Satan should buffet, though trials should come,
   Let this blest assurance control,
   That Christ has regarded my helpless estate,
   And hath shed His own blood for my soul.

3. My sin, oh, the bliss of this glorious thought,
   My sin not in part but the whole,
   Is nailed to the cross and I bear it no more,
   Praise the Lord, praise the Lord, oh my soul!

4. And, Lord, haste the day when the faith shall be sight,
   The clouds be rolled back as a scroll,
   The trump shall resound and the Lord shall descend,
   Even so it is well with my soul.

Jesus Is the Sweetest Name I Know

Words and Music by Lela Long

Strum Pattern: 3, 5
Pick Pattern: 1, 5

Verse
Prayerfully

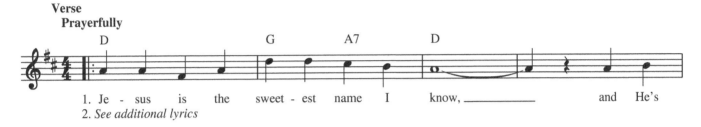

1. Je - sus is the sweet - est name I know, _____ and He's
2. *See additional lyrics*

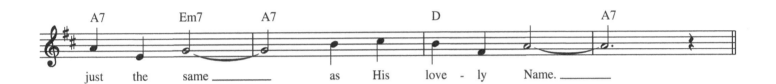

just the same _____ as His love - ly Name. _____

Chorus

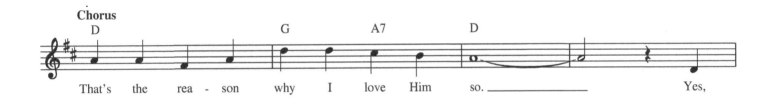

That's the rea - son why I love Him so. _____ Yes,

Je - sus is the sweet - est name I know. _____

Additional Lyrics

2. There's a name that cheers a broken heart,
   And He's mine I know as through life I go.

Jesus Paid It All

Words by Elvina M. Hall
Music by John T. Grape

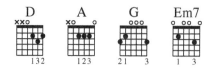

Strum Pattern: 9
Pick Pattern: 7

Verse
Moderately

1. I _____ hear the Sav - ior say; "Thy strength in - deed is small. Child of
2., 3., 4. *See additional lyrics*

weak - ness, watch and pray; find in Me thine all in all."

Chorus

Je - sus paid it all; all to Him I owe.

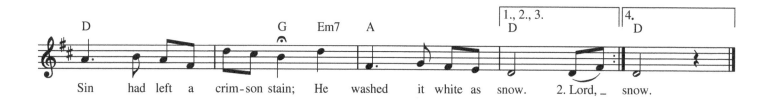

Sin had left a crim-son stain; He washed it white as snow. 2. Lord, _ snow.

Additional Lyrics

2. Lord, now indeed I find
   Thy pow'r, and Thine alone
   Can change the leper's spots
   And melt the heart of stone.

3. For nothing good have I
   Whereby Thy grace to claim;
   I'll wash my garments white
   In the blood of Calv'ry's Lamb.

4. And when before the throne
   I stand in Him complete,
   "Jesus died my soul to save,"
   My lips shall still repeat.

Joshua
(Fit the Battle of Jericho)

African-American Spiritual

Strum Pattern: 1, 2
Pick Pattern: 1, 4

Additional Lyrics

2. Way up to the walls of Jericho
   He marched with a spear in hand.
   "Go blow the ram's horn," Joshua cried,
   "Cause the battle is in my hands."

3. Then the lamb, ram, sheep horns began to blow
   And the trumpets began to sound;
   And Joshua commanded the children to shout
   And the walls come tumblin' down.

Just a Closer Walk With Thee

Traditional
Arranged by Kenneth Morris

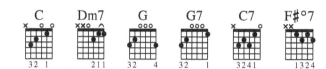

Strum Pattern: 4
Pick Pattern: 1

Verse
Moderately slow

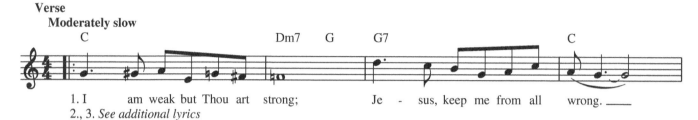

1. I am weak but Thou art strong; Je - sus, keep me from all wrong. ____
2., 3. *See additional lyrics*

I'll be sat - is - fied as long ____ as I walk, let me walk close to Thee.

Chorus

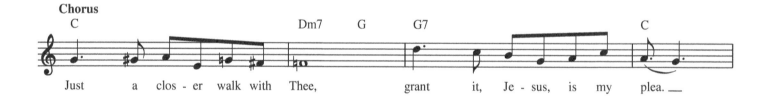

Just a clos - er walk with Thee, grant it, Je - sus, is my plea. ____

Dai - ly walk-ing close to Thee, ____ let it be, dear Lord, let it be. be.

Additional Lyrics

2. Through this world of toil and snares,
   If I falter, Lord, who cares?
   Who with me my burden shares?
   None but Thee, dear Lord, none but Thee.

3. When my feeble life is o'er,
   Time for me will be no more;
   Guide me gently, safely o'er
   To Thy kingdom shore, to Thy shore.

Just As I Am

Words by Charlotte Elliott
Music by William B. Bradbury

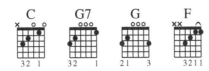

Strum Pattern: 7, 8
Pick Pattern: 7, 8

Verse
Moderately slow

1. Just __ as I am, __ with - out __ one plea but
2. – 5. *See additional lyrics*

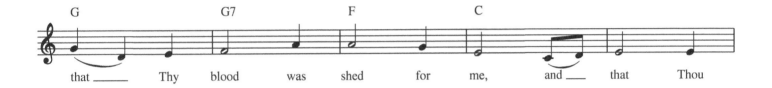

that __ Thy blood was shed for me, and __ that Thou

bidd'st __ me come to Thee, __ O Lamb of God, __ I

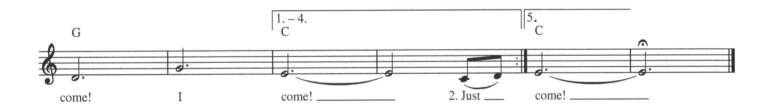

come! I come! __ 2. Just __ come! __

Additional Lyrics

2. Just as I am, and waiting not
   To rid my soul of one dark blot,
   To Thee whose blood can cleanse each spot,
   O Lamb of God, I come! I come!

3. Just as I am, though tossed about
   With many a conflict, many a doubt,
   Fightings and fears within, without,
   O Lamb of God, I come! I come!

4. Just as I am, poor, wretched, blind
   Sight, riches, healing of the mind.
   Yeah, all I need in Thee to find
   O Lamb of God, I come! I come!

5. Just as I am, Thou wilt receive,
   Wilt welcome, pardon, cleanse, relieve;
   Because Thy promise I believe,
   O Lamb of God, I come! I come!

The King Is Coming

Words by William J. and Gloria Gaither and Charles Millhuff
Music by William J. Gaither

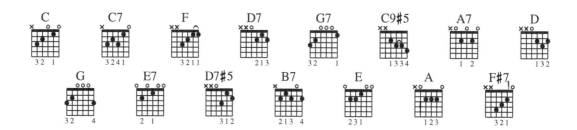

Strum Pattern: 7, 8
Pick Pattern: 7, 8

Verse
Mysteriously

1. The mar - ket place is emp-ty, no more traf-fic in the streets; all the build - ers' tools are si-lent, no more

time to har-vest wheat. Bu-sy house-wives cease their la-bors, in the court - room no de - bate; work on

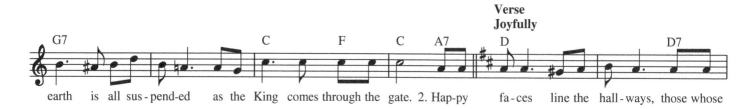

Verse
Joyfully

earth is all sus-pend-ed as the King comes through the gate. 2. Hap-py fa - ces line the hall-ways, those whose

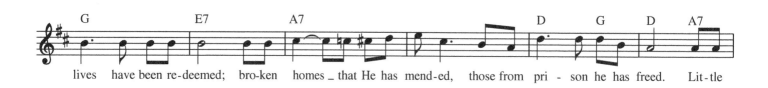

lives have been re-deemed; bro-ken homes _ that He has mend-ed, those from pri - son he has freed. Lit-tle

chil-dren and the a - ged hand in hand stand all a - glow, who were crip-pled, bro-ken, ru-ined, clad in

gar - ments white as snow. 3. I can hear the char-iots rum-ble, I can see the march-ing throng; the

flur - ry of God's trump-ets spell the end of sin and wrong. Re-gal robes are now un - fold-ing, Heav-en's

grand - stands all in place; Heav-en's choir is now as - sem-bled, start to sing "A-maz-ing Grace." Oh, ___ the

Chorus

King ___ is com-ing! The King ___ is com-ing! I just heard the trump-et sound-ing and

now His face I see. Oh, ___ the King ___ is com-ing! The King ___ is com-ing! Praise

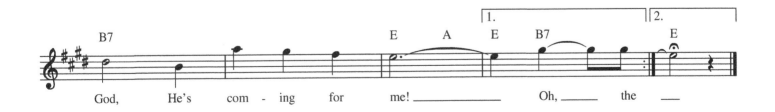

God, He's com - ing for me! ___ Oh, ___ the ___

Lamb of Glory

Words and Music by Greg Nelson and Phill McHugh

Strum Pattern: 8
Pick Pattern: 8

Verse
Slowly

1. Hear the sto - ry ___ from God's Word ___ that kings and priests and
2. *See additional lyrics*

proph - ets ___ heard: there would be a sac - ri - fice ___ and

blood would flow ___ to pay sin's price. Pre - cious Lamb of

glo - ry, love's most won - d'rous sto - ry, heart of

God's re - demp - tion of man, wor - ship the Lamb of glo -

ry. ___ glo - ry to the Lamb, pure as snow I

stand, wor-ship-ping the Lamb of glo - ry. With the saints ___ I will

stand ___ in e - ter - ni - ty, giv-ing thanks ___ to the Lamb ___ of glo -

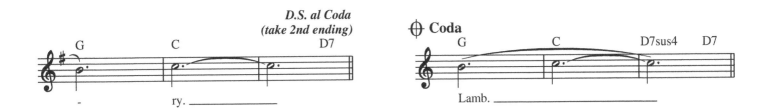

D.S. al Coda
(take 2nd ending)

Coda

- ry. ___

Lamb. ___

Outro-Chorus

Pre - cious Lamb of glo - ry, love's most won - d'rous

sto - ry, heart of God's re - demp - tion ___ of man, glo - ry to the

Lamb, pure as snow I stand, ___ wor-ship-ping the Lamb of glo -

ry. ___ Glo - ry! ___

Additional Lyrics

2. On the cross God loved the world,
While all the powers of hell were hurled.
No one there could understand
The One they saw was Christ the Lamb.

Leaning on the Everlasting Arms

Words by Elisha A. Hoffman
Music by Anthony J. Showalter

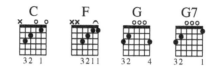

Strum Pattern: 4, 5
Pick Pattern: 1, 3

Verse
Confidently

1. What a fel - low - ship, what a joy di - vine, lean - ing on the ev - er - last - ing arms.
2. *See additional lyrics*

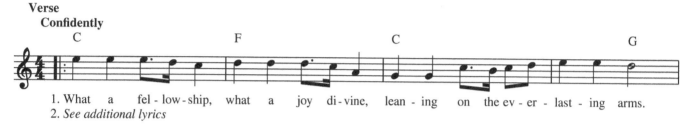

What a bless - ed - ness, what a peace is mine, lean - ing on the ev - er - last - ing arms.

Chorus

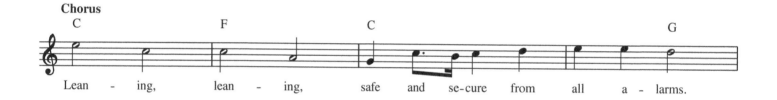

Lean - ing, lean - ing, safe and se - cure from all a - larms.

Lean - ing, lean - ing, lean - ing on the ev - er - last - ing arms. last - ing arms.

Additional Lyrics

2. Oh, how sweet to walk in this pilgrim way,
   Leaning on the everlasting arms.
   Oh, how bright the path grows from day to day.
   Leaning on the everlasting arms.

Let Us Break Bread Together

Traditional Spiritual

Strum Pattern: 3
Pick Pattern: 3

Verse
Moderately

1. Let us break bread to-geth-er on our knees, (On our knees.) let us
2., 3. *See additional lyrics*

break bread to - geth - er on our knees. (On our knees.) When I

Chorus

fall on my knees with my face to the ris - ing sun, oh

Lord, have mer - cy on me. (On me.) 2. Let us me.)

Additional Lyrics

2. Let us drink the cup together on our knees.
   (On our knees.)
   Let us drink the cup together on our knees.
   (On our knees.)

3. Let us praise God together on our knees.
   (On our knees.)
   Let us praise God together on our knees.
   (On our knees.)

Life's Railway to Heaven

Words by M.E. Abbey
Music by Charles D. Tillman

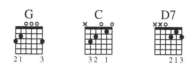

Strum Pattern: 7, 8
Pick Pattern: 7, 8

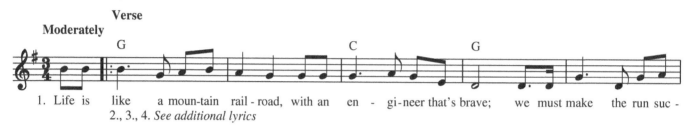

1. Life is like a moun-tain rail-road, with an en - gi-neer that's brave; we must make the run suc -
2., 3., 4. *See additional lyrics*

cess-ful from the cra - dle to the grave. Watch the curves, the fills, the tun-nels; nev-er fal - ter, nev-er quail; keep your

Chorus

hand up-on the throt-tle and your eye up-on the rail. Bless-ed Sav - ior, Thou wilt guide us, till we

reach that bliss-ful shore; where the an - gels wait to join us in Thy praise for-ev-er-more. 2. You will more.

Additional Lyrics

2. You will roll up grades of trial,
You will cross the bridge of strife;
See that Christ is your conductor
On this lightning train of life.
Always mindful of obstruction,
Do your duty, never fail;
Keep your hand upon the throttle
And your eye upon the rail.

3. You will often find obstructions,
Look for storms of wind and rain;
On a fill, or curve, or trestle,
They will almost ditch your train.
Put your trust alone in Jesus;
Never falter, never fail;
Keep your hand upon the throttle,
And your eye upon the rail.

4. As you roll across the trestle,
Spanning Jordan's swelling tide,
You behold the Union Depot,
Into which your train will glide.
There you'll meet the Superintendent
God the Father, God the Son,
With the hearty joyous plaudit,
"Weary pilgrim, welcome home!"

The Lighthouse

Words and Music by Ronnie Hinson

Strum Pattern: 3, 4
Pick Pattern: 1, 3

Verse

Slowly

1. There's a light-house on the hill-side that o-ver-look's life's sea. When I'm
2. *See additional lyrics*

tossed it sends out a light, _____ that I might see; and the

light that shines in dark-ness, now will safe-ly lead us o'er. _____ If it

was-n't for the light-house, my ship would be no more. And I thank

Chorus

God for the light-house, I owe my life to Him; for

Je-sus is the light-house and from the rocks of sin He has

shone a light a-round me that I could clear-ly see. If it

was-n't for the light-house, where would this ship be? 2. Ev-'ry- be?

Additional Lyrics

2. Ev'rybody that lives about us says, "Tear that lighthouse down;
   The big ships don't sail this way anymore, there's no use of it standing 'round,"
   Then my mind goes back to that stormy night, when just in time I saw the light,
   Yes, the light from that old lighthouse, that stands up there on the hill.

The Lily of the Valley

Words by Charles W. Fry
Music by William S. Hays

Strum Pattern: 3, 4
Pick Pattern: 1, 3

Verse

Moderately

1. I have found a friend in Je-sus, He's ev-'ry-thing to me, He's the
2., 3. *See additional lyrics*

fair-est of ten thou-sand to my soul. The ___ Lil-y of the Val-ley, in

Him a-lone I see all I need to cleanse and make me ful-ly whole. In

sor-row He's my com-fort, in trou-ble He's my stay; He ___ tells me ev-'ry care on Him to

Chorus

roll. He's the Lil-y of the Val-ley, the Bright and Morn-ing Star. He's the

1., 2.
fair-est of ten thou-sand to my soul. 2. He ___ soul.

3.

Additional Lyrics

2. He all my grief has taken, and all my sorrows borne.
In temptation He's my strong and mighty tower;
I have all for Him forsaken, all my idols torn.
From my heart, and now He keeps me by His power.
Though all the world forsake me,
And Satan tempt me sore,
Through Jesus I shall safely reach the goal.

3. He will never, never leave me, nor yet forsake me here,
While I live by faith and do His blessed will.
A wall of fire about me, I've nothing now to fear,
With His manna He my hungry soul shall fill.
Then sweeping up to glory
To see His blessed face,
Where rivers of delight shall ever roll.

Little Is Much When God Is in It

Words by Mrs. F.W. Suffield and Dwight Brock
Music by Mrs. F.W. Suffield

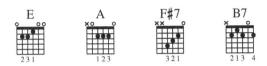

Strum Pattern: 9
Pick Pattern: 9

Verse
Moderately

1. In the har - vest field now rip - ened, there is work for all to do; hark, the
2., 3., 4. *See additional lyrics*

voice of God is call - ing, to the har - vest call - ing you. Lit - tle is

Chorus

much when God is in it; la - bor not for wealth or fame. There's a

crown, and you can win it if you go in Je - sus' name. 2. Does the name.

Additional Lyrics

2. Does the place you've called to labor seem so small and little known?
   It is great if God is in it, and He'll not forget His own.

3. Are you laid aside from service, body worn from toil and care?
   You can still be in the battle in the sacred place of prayer.

4. When the conflict here is ended and our race on earth is run;
   He will say, if we are faithful, "Welcome home, my child, well done."

The Longer I Serve Him

Words and Music by William J. Gaither

Strum Pattern: 7, 8
Pick Pattern: 7, 8

Verse
Reflectively

1. Since I start - ed for the King - dom, since my
2. *See additional lyrics*

life He con - trols, _____ since I gave my heart to

Je - sus, the long - er I serve _ Him, _____ the sweet - er He grows. _____ The

Chorus

long - er I serve Him, the sweet - er He grows. _____ The more that I love Him, more

love He be - stows. Each day is like heav - en, my heart o - ver - flows; the

long - er I serve _ Him, _____ the sweet - er He grows. grows.

Additional Lyrics

2. Ev'ry need He is supplying,
   Plenteous grace He bestows,
   Ev'ry day my way gets brighter;
   The longer I serve Him, the sweeter He grows.

Love Lifted Me

Words by James Rowe

Music by Howard E. Smith

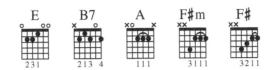

Strum Pattern: 8
Pick Pattern: 8

Verse

Moderately fast

1. I was sink-ing deep in sin, far from the peace-ful shore, ver-y deep-ly
2., 3. *See additional lyrics*

stained with-in, sink-ing to rise no more. But the Mas-ter of the sea

heard my des-pair-ing cry, from the wa-ters lift-ed me; now safe am I.

Chorus

Love lift-ed me! Love lift-ed me! When noth-ing else could help,

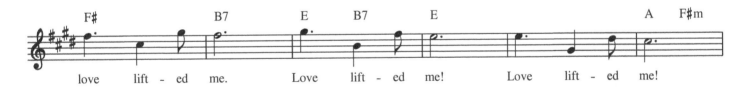

love lift-ed me. Love lift-ed me! Love lift-ed me!

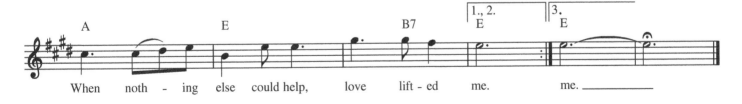

When noth-ing else could help, love lift-ed me. me. _____

Additional Lyrics

2. All my heart to Him I give, ever to Him I'll cling,
   In His blessed presence live, ever His praises sing;
   Love so mighty and so true merits my soul's best songs;
   Faithful, loving service, too to Him belongs.

3. Souls in danger, look above Jesus completely saves,
   He will lift you by His love out of the angry waves;
   He's the Master of the sea, billows His will obey;
   He your Savior wants to be, be saved today.

The Love of God

Words and Music by Frederick M. Lehman

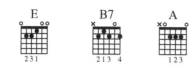

Strum Pattern: 9
Pick Pattern: 8

Verse

Moderately

1. The love of God is great-er far ___ than tongue or pen can ev - er tell; it goes be -
2., 3. *See additional lyrics*

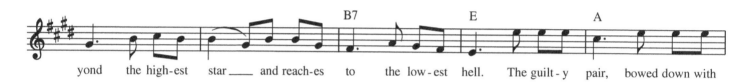

yond the high-est star ___ and reach-es to the low-est hell. The guilt - y pair, bowed down with

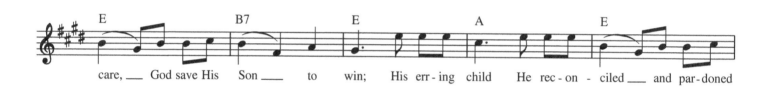

care, ___ God save His Son ___ to win; His err - ing child He rec - on - ciled ___ and par-doned

Chorus

from ___ his sin. O love of God, how rich and pure! ___ How meas - ure - less ___ and

strong! It shall for - ev - er-more en - dure, ___ the saints' and an - gels' song. 2. When years of song.

Additional Lyrics

2. When years of time shall pass away and earthly thrones and kingdoms fall,
   When men, who here refuse to pray, on rocks and hills and mountains call;
   God's love so sure shall still endure, all measureless and strong.
   Redeeming grace to Adam's race, the saints and angels' song.

3. Could we with ink the ocean fill and were the skies of parchment made,
   Were ev'ry stalk on earth a quill, and ev'ry man a scribe by trade;
   To write the love of God above would drain the ocean dry,
   Nor could the scroll contain the whole, though stretched from sky to sky.

Mansion Over the Hilltop

Words and Music by Ira F. Stanphill

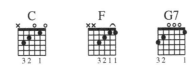

Strum Pattern: 3, 4
Pick Pattern: 3, 6

Moderately

Verse

1. I'm sat-is-fied with _____ just a cot-tage be - low, _____ a lit-tle
2., 3. *See additional lyrics*

sil - ver _____ and a lit-tle gold. _____ But in that cit - y _____ where the ran-somed will

shine, _____ I want a gold one _____ that's sil - ver _ lined. _____ I've got a

Chorus

man - sion _____ just o-ver the hill - top, in that bright land where _____ we'll nev-er grow

old. _____ And some day yon - der _____ we will nev-er more wan - der, but walk the

1., 2.

3.

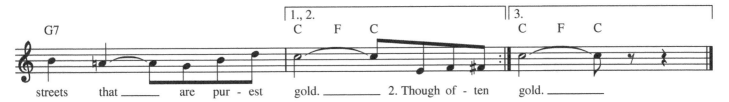

streets that _____ are pur - est gold. _____ 2. Though of - ten gold. _____

Additional Lyrics

2. Though often tempted, tormented and tested,
   And, like the prophet, my pillow a stone.
   And though I find here no permanent dwelling,
   I know He'll give me a mansion my own.

3. Don't think me poor or deserted or lonely,
   I'm not discouraged, I'm heaven-bound.
   I'm just a pilgrim in search of a city,
   I want a mansion, a harp and a crown.

Midnight Cry

Words and Music by Greg Day and Chuck Day

Strum Pattern: 1
Pick Pattern: 2

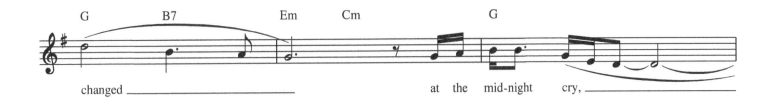

changed _____ at the mid-night cry, _____

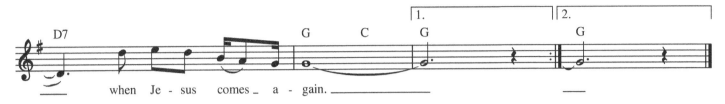

_____ when Je - sus comes _ a - gain. _____

Additional Lyrics

2. I looked around me, I see prophecies fulfilling;
   And the signs of the times, they're appearing everywhere.
   I can almost hear the Father as He says,
   "Son, go get Your children,"
   And at the midnight cry, the Bride of Christ will rise.

Put Your Hand in the Hand

Words and Music by Gene MacLellan

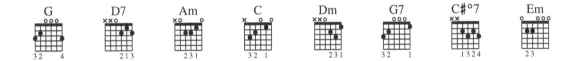

Strum Pattern: 2, 3
Pick Pattern: 1, 3

Put your hand in the hand of the Man who stilled the wa - ter, _____

_____ put your hand in the hand of the Man who calmed _ the

sea. _____ Take a look at your - self and a

you can look at oth-ers dif-f'rent-ly, by put-tin' your

hand in the hand of the Man from Gal-i - lee. _____ 1. Ev - 'ry
2. *See additional lyrics*

Verse

time I look in - to the Ho - ly Book I wan-na trem - ble _____

____ when I read a-bout the part where a Car-pen-ter cleared the

Tem - ple; _____ for the buy-ers and the sell-ers were

no dif - f'rent fel - las than what I pro-fess to be, and it

caus-es me shame to know I'm not the man that I should be! _____ Put your

D.S. al Coda

through. _____ Put your

Coda

lee. _____

Additional Lyrics

2. Mama taught me how to pray before I reached the age of seven;
When I'm down on my knees, that's-a when I'm close to heaven.
Daddy lived his life with two kids and a wife and he did what he could do.
And he showed me enough of what it takes t' get you through.

My God Is Real
(Yes, God Is Real)

Words and Music by Kenneth Morris

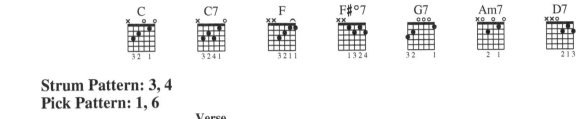

C   C7   F   F#°7   G7   Am7   D7

Strum Pattern: 3, 4
Pick Pattern: 1, 6

Verse

Slowly

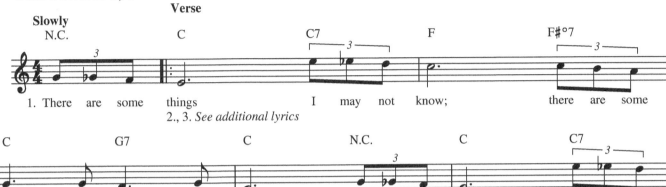

1. There are some things I may not know;
2., 3. *See additional lyrics*

plac - es I can't go. But I am sure of this one

thing: that God is real for I can feel Him deep with - in. My God is

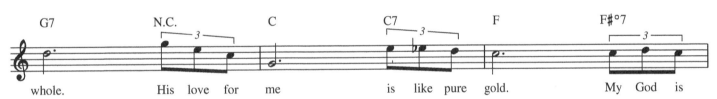

real, real in my soul; my God is real for He has washed and made me

whole. His love for me is like pure gold. My God is

C   G7   1., 2. C   N.C.   3. C   F   C

real for I can feel Him in my soul. 2. Some folks may soul.

Additional Lyrics

2. Some folks may doubt, some folks may scorn;
   All can desert and leave me alone.
   But as for me I'll take God's part,
   For God is real and I can feel Him in my heart.

3. I cannot tell just how you felt
   When Jesus took your sins away.
   But since that day, yes since that hour,
   God has been real for I can feel Him in my heart.

More Than Wonderful

Words and Music by Lanny Wolfe

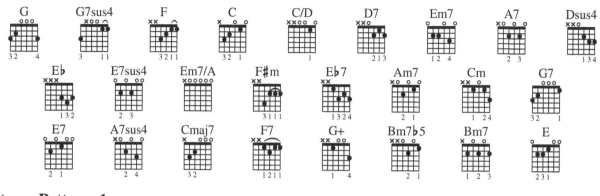

Strum Pattern: 1
Pick Pattern: 2

Verse
Slowly

1. He prom-ised us __ that He would be __ a Coun - sel-or, a Might-y God __ and a Prince _ of

Peace. _____ He prom-ised us __ that He would be __ a Fa - ther, and would

love us with a love _ that would _ not _ cease. 2. Well, _ I tried Him and I found His prom-is - es are true; _ He's
3. *See additional lyrics*

ev - 'ry-thing _ He said that He _ would _ be. The fin - est words _ I know could not be -

gin to _ tell just _ how much Je - sus real - ly means _ to me. For

Chorus

He's more won - der-ful than my mind can con-ceive, He's more won - der-ful than my

heart can be-lieve, He goes be - yond my high-est hopes and fond - est dreams. _____

Additional Lyrics

3. I stand amazed to think the King of Glory
   Would come to live within the heart of man.
   I marvel just to know He really loves me
   When I think of who He is and who I am.

My Savior First of All

Words by Fanny J. Crosby
Music by John R. Sweney

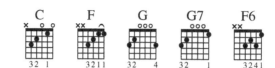

Additional Lyrics

2. O the soul thrilling rapture when I view His blessed face
   And the luster of His kindly beaming eye;
   How my full heart will praise Him for the mercy, love and grace
   That prepare for me a mansion in the sky.

3. O the dear ones in glory, how They beckon me to come,
   And our parting at the river I recall;
   To the sweet vales of Eden They will sing my welcome home,
   But I long to meet my Savior first of all.

4. Through the gates to the city in a robe of spotless white,
   He will lead me where no tears will ever fall
   In the glad song of ages I shall mingle with delight,
   But I long to meet my Savior first of all.

A New Name in Glory

Words and Music by C. Austin Miles

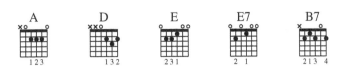

Strum Pattern: 1
Pick Pattern: 2

Verse
Moderately

1. I was once a sin-ner, but I came, par-don to re-ceive from my Lord. ___
2., 3. *See additional lyrics*

This was free-ly giv-en, and I found that He al-ways kept His word. There's a

Chorus

new name writ-ten down _ in glo-ry, ___ and it's mine, O yes, it's mine! And the

white robed an-gels sing the sto-ry, ___ "A sin-ner has come home." For there's a

new name writ-ten down _ in glo-ry, ___ and it's mine, O yes it's mine! With my

sins for-giv-en I am bound for heav-en, nev-er-more to roam. roam.

Additional Lyrics

2. I was humbly kneeling at the cross
   Fearing naught but God's angry frown,
   When the heavens opened and I saw
   That my name was written down.

3. In the Book 'tis written, "Saved by grace."
   Oh, the joy that came to my soul!
   Now I am forgiven and I know
   By the blood I am made whole.

My Tribute

Words and Music by Andraé Crouch

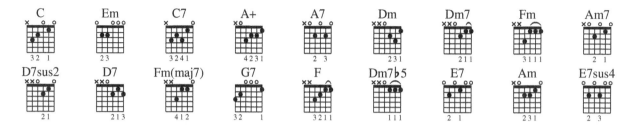

Strum Pattern: 4, 5
Pick Pattern: 5, 6

Verse
Slowly

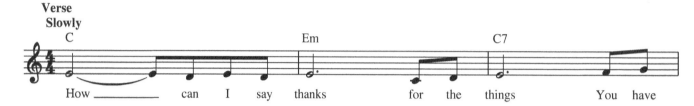

How _____ can I say thanks for the things You have

done for me? Things _____ so un-de-served, yet You

give _____ to prove your love for me. The voic-es of a mil-lion

an-gels _____ could not ex-press _____ my grat-i-tude; all that I

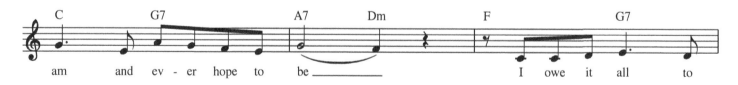

am and ev-er hope to be _____ I owe it all to

Chorus
Brightly

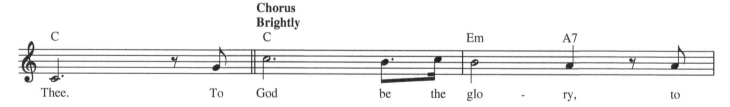

Thee. To God be the glo-ry, to

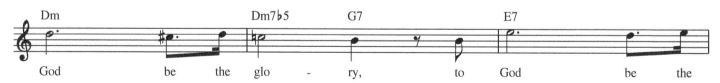

God be the glo-ry, to God be the

glo - ry for the things He has done. With His

blood He has saved me, with His pow'r He has raised me, to

God be the glo - ry for the things He has done. Just let me

live my life _____ let it be pleas - ing, Lord to

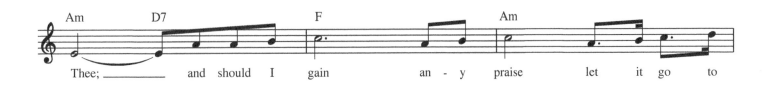

Thee; _____ and should I gain an - y praise let it go to

Outro

cal - va - ry. With His blood He has saved me, with His

pow'r He has raised me, to God be the glo - ry for the

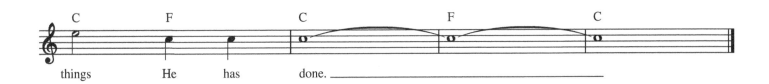

things He has done. _____

Nothing But the Blood

Words and Music by Robert Lowry

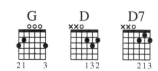

Strum Pattern: 4
Pick Pattern: 1

Verse
Moderately slow

1. What can wash a-way my sin? Noth-ing but the blood of Je - sus;
2., 3., 4. *See additional lyrics*

what can make me whole a - gain? Noth-ing but the blood of Je - sus.

Chorus

O pre - cious is the flow that makes me white as snow; ___

no oth - er fount I know, noth-ing but the blood of Je - sus. Je - sus.

Additional Lyrics

2. For my pardon this I see,
   Nothing but the blood of Jesus;
   For my cleansing, this my plea,
   Nothing but the blood of Jesus.

3. Nothing can for sin atone,
   Nothing but the blood of Jesus;
   Naught of good that I have done,
   Nothing but the blood of Jesus.

4. This is all my hope and peace,
   Nothing but the blood of Jesus;
   This is all my righteousness,
   Nothing but the blood of Jesus.

Oh, How I Love Jesus

Words by Frederick Whitfield
Traditional American Melody

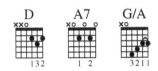

Strum Pattern: 8
Pick Pattern: 8

Verse
Moderately

1. There is a name __ I love to hear, I love to sing __ its worth; __ it
2., 3., 4. *See additional lyrics*

sounds like mu - sic in my ear, the sweet - est name on earth. __

Chorus

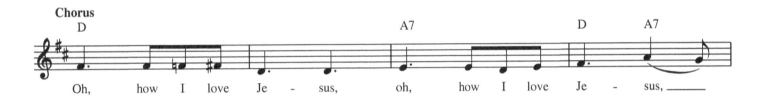

Oh, how I love Je - sus, oh, how I love Je - sus, __

oh, how I love Je - sus, be - cause __ He first loved me. 2. It me.

Additional Lyrics

2. It tells me of a Savior's love,
   Who died to set me free;
   It tells me of His precious blood,
   The sinner's perfect plea.

3. It tells me what my Father hath
   In store for ev'ry day;
   And though I tread a darksome path,
   Yields sunshine all the way.

4. It tells of One whose loving heart
   Can feel my deepest woe,
   Who in each sorrow bears a part
   That none can bear below.

The Old Rugged Cross

Words and Music by Rev. George Bennard

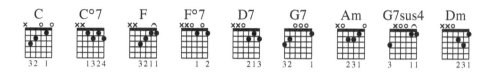

C   C°7   F   F°7   D7   G7   Am   G7sus4   Dm

Strum Pattern: 8
Pick Pattern: 8

Verse
Expressively

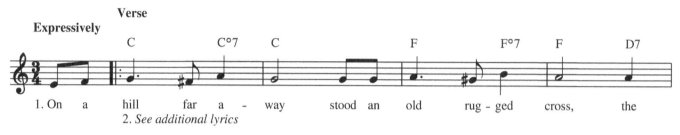

1. On a hill far a - way stood an old rug - ged cross, the
2. *See additional lyrics*

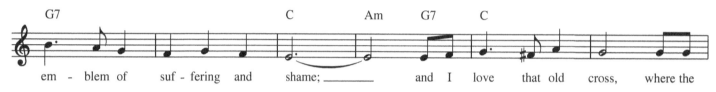

em - blem of suf - fering and shame; _____ and I love that old cross, where the

dear - est and best for a world of lost sin - ners was slain. _____ So I'll

Chorus

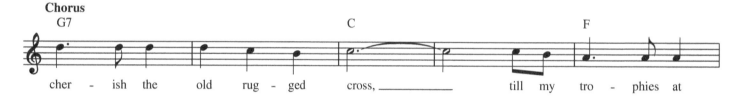

cher - ish the old rug - ged cross, _____ till my tro - phies at

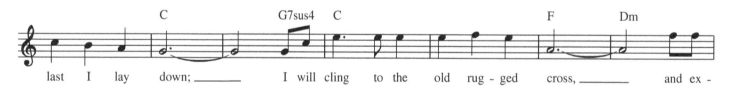

last I lay down; _____ I will cling to the old rug - ged cross, _____ and ex -

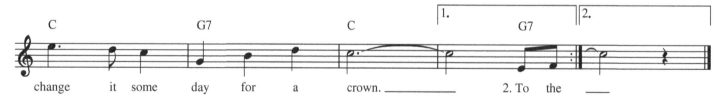

change it some day for a crown. _____ 2. To the _____

Additonal Lyrics

2. To the old rugged cross I will ever be true,
   Its shame and reproach gladly bear;
   Then He'll call me some day to my home far away,
   Where His glory forever I'll share.

On Jordan's Stormy Banks

Words by Samuel Stennett
Traditional American Melody arranged by Rigdon M. McIntosh

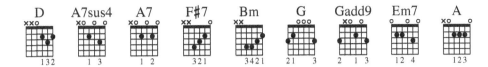

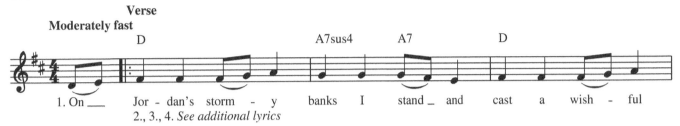

Strum Pattern: 3
Pick Pattern: 3

Verse
Moderately fast

1. On ___ Jor - dan's storm - y banks I stand ___ and cast a wish - ful
2., 3., 4. *See additional lyrics*

eye to ___ Ca - naan's ___ fair and hap - py land where ___ my pos - ses - sions

Chorus

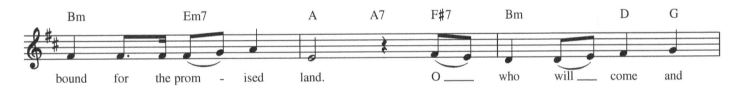

lie. I am bound for the prom - ised land, _____ I am

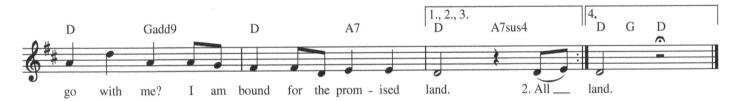

bound for the prom - ised land. O ___ who will ___ come and

go with me? I am bound for the prom - ised land. 2. All ___ land.

Additional Lyrics

2. All o'er these wide extended plains
   Shines one eternal day.
   There God the Son forever reigns
   And scatters night away.

3. No chilling winds nor pois'nous breath
   Can reach that healthful shore;
   Sickness and sorrow, pain and death
   Are felt and feared no more.

4. When shall I reach that happy place
   And be forever blest?
   When shall I see my Father's face
   And in His bosom rest?

(There'll Be) Peace in the Valley (For Me)

Words and Music by Thomas A. Dorsey

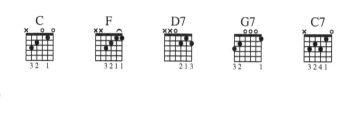

Strum Pattern: 7, 9
Pick Pattern: 7, 9

Verse

Moderately

1. I am tir - ed and wea - ry but I must toil on, till the Lord comes to
2. *See additional lyrics*

call me a - way, where the morn - ing is bright and the

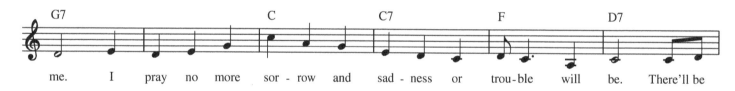

Lamb is the light and the night is as fair as the day. There'll be

Chorus

peace in the val - ley for me some - day. There'll be peace in the val - ley for

me. I pray no more sor - row and sad - ness or trou - ble will be. There'll be

peace in the val - ley for me. 2. There'll be me.

Additional Lyrics

2. There'll be flow'rs that are blooming, the grass will be green.
And the skies will be clear and serene.
The sun ever shines, giving one endless beam.
And no clouds there will ever be seen.

Precious Lord, Take My Hand
(Take My Hand, Precious Lord)

Words and Music by Thomas A. Dorsey

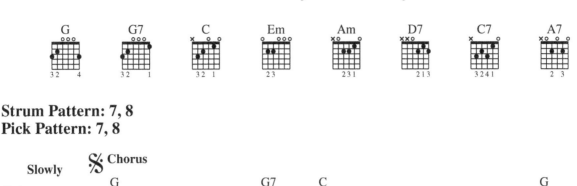

Strum Pattern: 7, 8
Pick Pattern: 7, 8

Slowly

Chorus

Pre-cious Lord, take my hand, lead me on, let me stand, _ I am tired, _ I am

weak, I am worn. ___ Through the storm, through the night, lead me on to the

To Coda

light. _ Take my hand, _ pre-cious Lord, ___ lead me home. ___ 1. When my
2. *See additional lyrics*

Verse

way grows_ drear, pre-cious Lord, lin-ger near. _ When my life _ is _ al-most _

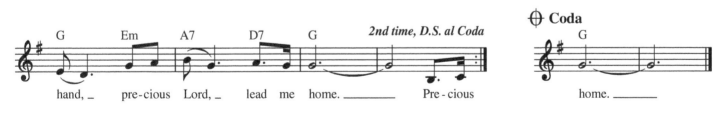

gone, ___ hear my cry, hear my_ call, _ hold_ my hand lest I fall. _ Take_ my

2nd time, D.S. al Coda   **Coda**

hand, _ pre-cious Lord, _ lead me home. ___ Pre-cious   home. ___

Additional Lyrics

2. When the darkness appears and the night draws near
   And the day is past and gone,
   At the river I stand, guide my feet, hold my hand.
   Take my hand, precious Lord, lead me home.

Precious Memories

Words and Music by J.B.F. Wright

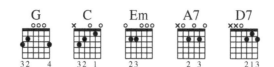

Strum Pattern: 3, 4
Pick Pattern: 4, 5

Verse
Slowly

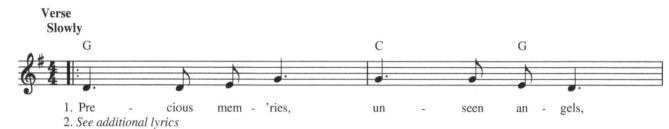

1. Pre - cious mem - 'ries, un - seen an - gels,
2. *See additional lyrics*

sent from some - where to my soul; how they lin - ger,

ev - er near me, and the sa - cred past un - fold.

Chorus

Pre - cious mem - 'ries, how they lin - ger, how they ev - er flood my

soul. _____ In the still - ness of the mid - night,

pre - cious sa - cred scenes un - fold. fold.

Additional Lyrics

2. Precious father, loving mother,
Fly across the lonely years;
To old home scenes of my childhood,
With fond memories appear.

Room at the Cross for You

Words and Music by Ira F. Stanphill

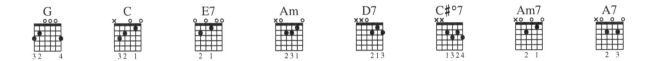

Strum Pattern: 8
Pick Pattern: 7

Verse
Moderately

1. The cross up-on which Je-sus died _____ is a shel-ter in which we can
2., 3. *See additional lyrics*

hide. _____ And its grace so free is suf-fi-cient for me, and

Chorus

deep is its foun-tain; as wide as the sea. There's room at the cross for

you. _____ There's room at the cross for you. _____ Though mil-lions have come, there's

still room for one. Yes, there's room at the cross for you. _____ 2. Though you.

Additional Lyrics

2. Though millions have found him a friend
   And have turned from the sins they have sinned,
   The Savior still waits to open the gates
   And welcome a sinner before it's too late.

3. The head of my Savior is strong
   And the love of my Savior is long.
   The sunshine or rain, through loss or in gain,
   The blood flows from Calvary to cleanse every stain.

Rise Again

Words and Music by Dallas Holm

Strum Pattern: 3, 4
Pick Pattern: 4, 5

Verse
Slowly

1. Go a - head, drive the nails ___ in my hands; laugh at me where you stand. Go a - head and say it is - n't me; the day ___ will come ___ when you ___ will see! 'Cause I'll (1., 2.) rise ___ a -

(3.) come ___ a -

gain; Ain't no pow'r on ___ earth can tie ___ me down..
gain; Ain't no pow'r on ___ earth can keep ___ me back. _

Yes, I'll rise ___ a - gain;
Yes, I'll come ___ a - gain;

To Coda 1 ⊕
To Coda 2 ⊕

death can't keep me ___ in the ground. ___ 2. Go a -
come to take my ___ peo - ple back. _

Rock of Ages

Words by Augstus M. Toplady
v.1,2,4 altered by Thomas Cotterill
Music by Thomas Hastings

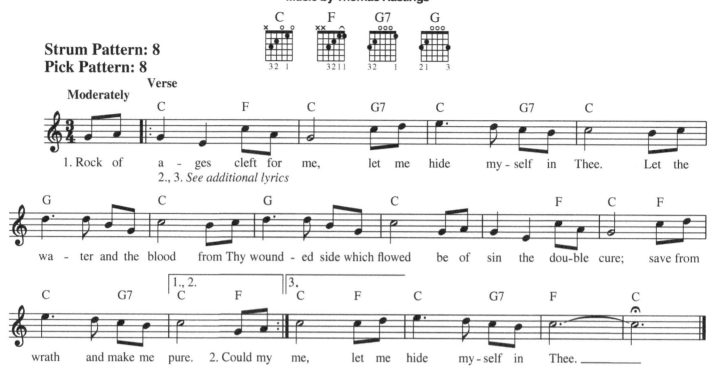

Strum Pattern: 8
Pick Pattern: 8

Verse
Moderately

1. Rock of a - ges cleft for me, let me hide my - self in Thee. Let the
2., 3. *See additional lyrics*

wa - ter and the blood from Thy wound - ed side which flowed be of sin the dou - ble cure; save from

wrath and make me pure. 2. Could my me, let me hide my - self in Thee. _____

Additional Lyrics

2. Could my tears forever flow,
Could my zeal no languor know?
These for sin could not atone,
Thou must save and Thou alone.
I my hand no price I bring,
Simply to Thy cross I cling.

3. While I draw this fleeting breath,
When my eyes shall close in death.
When I rise to worlds unknown,
And behold Thee on Thy throne.
Rock of ages cleft for me,
Let me hide myself in Thee,
Let me hide myself in Thee.

Tears Are a Language God Understands

Words and Music by Gordon Jensen

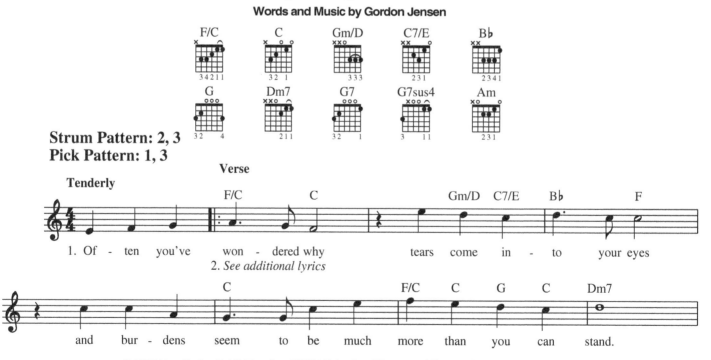

Strum Pattern: 2, 3
Pick Pattern: 1, 3

Verse
Tenderly

1. Of - ten you've won - dered why tears come in - to your eyes
2. *See additional lyrics*

and bur - dens seem to be much more than you can stand.

But God is stand - ing near, He sees your fall - ing tears;

tears are __ a lan - guage God un - der - stands.

Chorus

God sees the tears of a bro - ken - heart - ed soul,

He sees your _ tears and hears them when they fall.

God weeps _ a - long with man and takes him

by the hand; tears are __ a lan - guage God un - der -

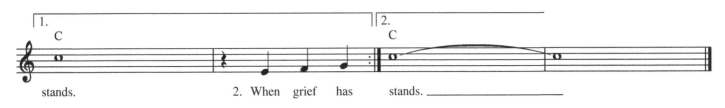

stands.   2. When grief has stands. _____

Additional Lyrics

2. When grief has left you low, it causes tears to flow,
   Things have not turned out the way that you had planned.
   But God won't forget you, His promises are true;
   Tears are a language God understands.

Shall We Gather at the River?

Words and Music by Robert Lowry

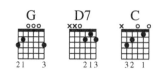

Strum Pattern: 3
Pick Pattern: 3

Verse
Moderately

1. Shall we gath - er at the riv - er, where bright an - gel feet have
2. – 5. *See additional lyrics*

trod; _____ with its crys - tal tide for - ev - er flow - ing

Chorus

from the __ throne of ___ God? Yes, we'll gath - er at the riv - er, the

beau - ti - ful, the beau - ti - ful ___ riv - er. Gath - er with the saints ___ at the

riv - er, that flows from the throne of _____ God. God.

Additional Lyrics

2. On the margin of the river,
   Washing up its silver spray,
   We shall walk and worship ever
   All the happy, golden day.

3. On the bosom of the river,
   Where the Saviour King we own,
   We shall meet and sorrow never
   'Neath the glory of the throne.

4. Ere we reach the shining river,
   Lay we ev'ry burden down.
   Grace our spirits will deliver,
   And provide a robe and crown.

5. Soon we'll reach the shining river,
   Soon our pilgrimage will cease;
   Soon our happy hearts will quiver
   With the melody of peace.

Since Jesus Came Into My Heart

Words by Rufus H. McDaniel
Music by Charles H. Gabriel

Strum Pattern: 4
Pick Pattern: 1

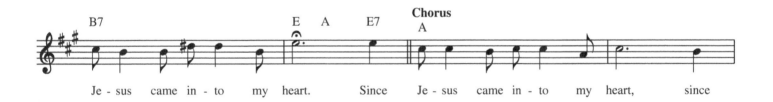

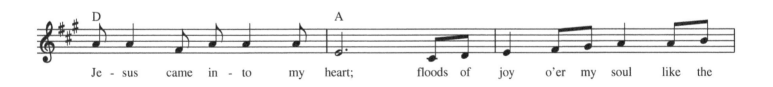

Soon and Very Soon

Words and Music by Andraé Crouch

Stepping on the Clouds

Words and Music by Linda Stalls

Sweet Beulah Land

Words and Music by Squire Parsons

Strum Pattern: 3
Pick Pattern: 3

Slowly

Verse

1. I'm kind of home - sick for a coun - try _____ to which _ I've _
2. *See additional lyrics*

nev - er been be - fore. _____ No _ sad good -

byes _____ will there be spo - ken _____ for time _ won't _

mat - ter an - y more. _____ Beu - lah

Chorus

land _____ I'm _ long - ing for _ you _____ and _ some _

day _____ on _ Thee _ I'll stand. _____ There my

home _____ shall _ be _ e - ter - nal Beu - lah land _____

_____ sweet _ Beu - lah land. _____ 2. I'm look - ing land.

Additional Lyrics

2. I'm looking now across the river
To where my faith will end in sight.
There's just a few more days to labor
Then I will take my heav'nly flight.

Sweet By and By

Words by Sanford Fillmore Bennett
Music by Joseph P. Webster

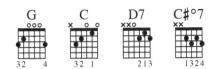

Strum Pattern: 2, 3
Pick Pattern: 3, 4

Verse

Cheerfully

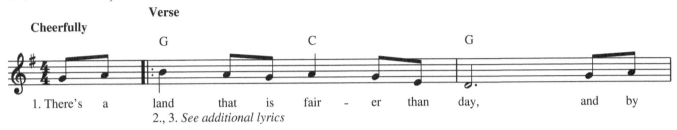

1. There's a land that is fair - er than day, and by
2., 3. *See additional lyrics*

faith we can see it a - far. For the Fa - ther waits o - ver the

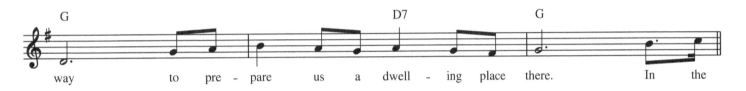

way to pre - pare us a dwell - ing place there. In the

Chorus

sweet by and by, we shall meet on that beau - ti - ful shore. In the

sweet by and by, we shall meet on that beau - ti - ful shore. 2. We shall shore.

Additional Lyrics

2. We shall sing on that beautiful shore
   The melodious songs of the blest.
   And our spirits shall sorrow no more,
   Not a sigh for the blessing of rest.

3. To our bountiful Father above
   We will offer the tribute of praise.
   For the glorious gift of His love,
   And the blessings that hallow our days.

Sweet, Sweet Spirit

By Doris Akers

Strum Pattern: 5
Pick Pattern: 5

Additional Lyrics

2. There are blessings you cannot receive
   'Til you know Him in His fullness and believe;
   You're the one to profit when you say,
   "I am going to walk with Jesus all the way."

There Is a Fountain

Words by William Cowper
Traditional American Melody
Arranged by Lowell Mason

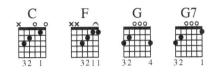

Strum Pattern: 2
Pick Pattern: 4

Verse
Moderately

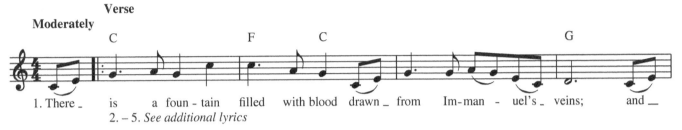

1. There _ is a foun-tain filled with blood drawn _ from Im-man - uel's _ veins; and _
2. – 5. *See additional lyrics*

sin - ners, plunged be - neath that flood, lose _ all their guilt - y stains, lose _

all their guilt - y stains, _____ lose all their guil - ty _ stains. And _

sin - ners, plunged be - neath that flood, lose _ all their guilt - y stains. 2. The _ grave.

Additional Lyrics

2. The dying thief rejoiced to see
   That fountain in his day;
   And there may I, though vile as he,
   Wash all my sins away,
   Wash all my sins away,
   Wash all my sins away.
   And there may I, though vile as he,
   Wash all my sins away.

3. Dear dying Lamb, Thy precious blood
   Shall never lose its power,
   Till all the ransomed Church of God
   Be saved, to sin no more,
   Be saved, to sin no more,
   Be saved, to sin no more.
   Till all the ransomed Church of God
   Be saved, to sin no more.

4. E'er since by faith, I saw the stream
   Thy flowing wounds supply,
   Redeeming love has been my theme,
   And shall be till I die,
   And shall be till I die,
   And shall be till I die.
   Redeeming love has been my theme,
   And shall be till I die.

5. Then in a nobler, sweeter song,
   I'll sing Thy power to save,
   When this poor lisping, stamm'ring tongue
   Lies silent in the grave,
   Lies silent in the grave,
   Lies silent in the grave.
   When this poor lisping, stamm'ring tongue
   Lies silent in the grave.

There Is Power in the Blood

Words and Music by Lewis E. Jones

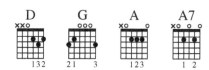

Strum Pattern: 3, 4
Pick Pattern: 1, 3

Verse
Brightly

1. Would you be free from the bur - den of sin? There's pow'r in the blood, pow'r in the blood;
2., 3., 4. *See additional lyrics*

would you o'er e - vil a vic - to - ry win? There's won - der - ful pow'r in the blood. There is

Chorus

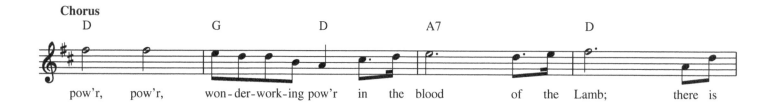

pow'r, pow'r, won - der-work-ing pow'r in the blood of the Lamb; there is

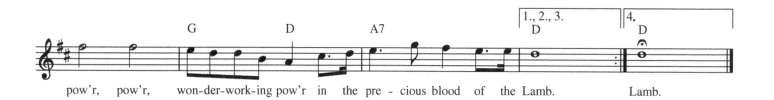

pow'r, pow'r, won - der-work-ing pow'r in the pre - cious blood of the Lamb. Lamb.

Additional Lyrics

2. Would you be free from your passion and pride?
There's pow'r in the blood, pow'r in the blood;
Come for a cleansing to Calvary's tide;
There's wonderful pow'r in the blood.

3. Would you be whiter, much whiter than snow?
There's pow'r in the blood, pow'r in the blood;
Sin stains are lost in its life giving flow;
There's wonderful pow'r in the blood.

4. Would you do service for Jesus your King?
There's pow'r in the blood, pow'r in the blood;
Would you live daily His praises to sing:
There's wonderful pow'r in the blood.

There's Something About That Name

Words by William J. and Gloria Gaither

Music by William J. Gaither

Strum Pattern: 9

Pick Pattern: 9

Recitation

Spoken: 2. *Jesus, the mere mention of His name can calm the storm, heal the broken, raise the dead.*
At the name of Jesus, I've seen sin-hardened men melted, derelicts transformed,
the lights of hope put back into the eyes of a hopeless child...

At the name of Jesus, hatred and bitterness turned to love and forgiveness, arguments cease.

I've heard a mother softly breathe His name at the bedside of a child delirious from fever,
and I've watched that little body grow quiet and the fevered brow cool.

I've sat beside a dying saint, her body racked with pain, who in those final fleeting seconds
summoned her last ounce of ebbing strength to whisper earth's sweetest name - Jesus. Jesus...

Emperors have tried to destroy it; philosophies have tried to stamp it out.
Tyrants have tried to wash it from the face of the earth with the very blood of those who claimed it. Yet still it stands.

And there shall be that final day when every voice that has ever uttered a sound -
every voice of Adam's race shall raise in one great mighty chorus to proclaim the name of Jesus -
for in that day "every knee shall bow and every tongue shall confess that Jesus Christ is Lord!!!"

Ah - so you see - it was not mere chance that caused the angel one night long ago to say to a virgin maiden,
"His name shall be called Jesus." Jesus - Jesus - Jesus. You know, there is something about that name...

'Tis So Sweet to Trust in Jesus

Words by Louisa M.R. Stead
Music by William J. Kirkpatrick

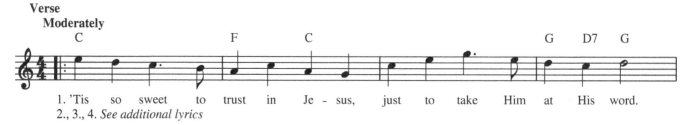

Strum Pattern: 1, 3
Pick Pattern: 2, 4

Verse
Moderately

1. 'Tis so sweet to trust in Je - sus, just to take Him at His word.
2., 3., 4. *See additional lyrics*

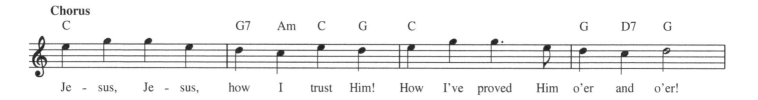

Just to rest up - on His prom - ise, just to know "Thus saith the Lord."

Chorus

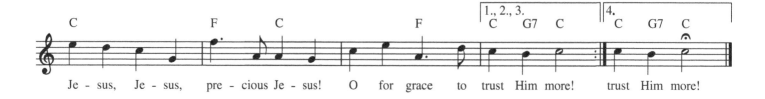

Je - sus, Je - sus, how I trust Him! How I've proved Him o'er and o'er!

Je - sus, Je - sus, pre - cious Je - sus! O for grace to trust Him more! trust Him more!

Additional Lyrics

2. O how sweet to trust in Jesus,
   Just to trust His cleansing blood,
   Just in simple faith to plunge me
   'Neath the healing, cleansing flood!

3. Yes, 'tis sweet to trust in Jesus,
   Just from sin and self to cease,
   Just from Jesus simply taking
   Life and rest and joy and peace.

4. I'm so glad I learned to trust Him,
   Precious Jesus, Savior, Friend;
   And I know that He is with me;
   Will be with me to the end.

Turn Your Radio On

Words and Music by Albert E. Brumley

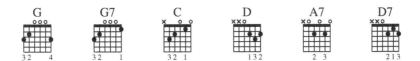

Strum Pattern: 5
Pick Pattern: 6

1. Come and lis-ten in to a ra-di-o sta-tion where the might-y hosts of heav-en sing, turn your ra-di-o
2., 3. *See additional lyrics*

on, _____ turn your ra-di-o on. If you want to

head the songs of Zi-on com-ing from the land of end-less spring, get in touch with

God, _____ turn your ra-di-o on. _____ Turn your ra-di-o

Chorus

on _____ and lis-ten to the mu-sic in the air, turn your ra-di-o

on, _____ heav-en's glo-ry share; _____ turn the lights down

low _____ and lis-ten to the Mas-ter's ra-di-o, get in touch with

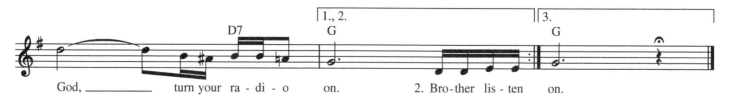

God, _____ turn your ra-di-o on. 2. Bro-ther lis-ten on.

1., 2. | **3.**

Additional Lyrics

2. Brother listen in to a gloryland chorus
   Listen to the glad hosanas roll
   Turn your radio on, turn your radio on.
   Get a little taste of joy awaiting
   Get a little heaven in your soul
   Get in touch with God, turn your radio on.

3. Listen to the songs of the fathers and mothers
   And the many friends gone on before,
   Turn your radio on, turn your radio on;
   Some eternal morning we shall meet them
   Over on the hallelujah shore,
   Get in touch with God, turn your radio on.

Victory in Jesus

Words and Music by E.M. Bartlett

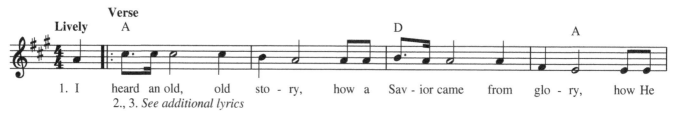

Strum Pattern: 2
Pick Pattern: 2

Verse

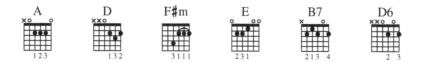

Lively   A

1. I heard an old, old sto-ry, how a Sav-ior came from glo-ry, how He
2., 3. *See additional lyrics*

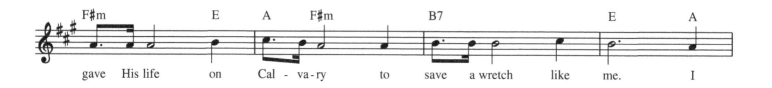

F#m   E   A   F#m   B7   E   A

gave His life on Cal-va-ry to save a wretch like me. I

heard a-bout His groan - ing, of His pre - cious blood's a - ton - ing, then

I re - pent - ed of my sins and won the vic - to - ry. Oh

Chorus

vic - to - ry in Je - sus, my Sav - ior for - ev - er, He

sought me and bought me with His re - deem - ing blood. He

loved me ere I knew Him, and all my love is due Him. He

plunged me to vic - to - ry be - neath the cleans - ing flood. 2. I flood.

Additional Lyrics

2. I heard about His healing, of His cleansing pow'r revealing,
   How He made the lame to walk again and caused the blind to see;
   And then I cried, "Dear Jesus, come and heal my broken spirit."
   And somehow Jesus came and brought to me the victory.

3. I heard about a mansion He has built for me in glory,
   And I heard about the streets of gold beyond the crystal sea;
   About the angels singing and the old redemption story.
   And some sweet day I'll sing up there the song of victory.

The Unclouded Day

Words and Music by J.K. Alwood

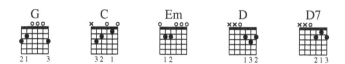

*Strum Pattern: 3
*Pick Pattern: 3

Moderately

1. Oh they tell me of a home far be - yond the skies, oh they tell me of a home far a - way; oh they

2., 3., 4. *See additional lyrics*

*Use Pattern 10 for 2/4 measures.

tell me of a home where no storm-clouds rise, oh they tell me of an un - cloud-ed day.

Chorus

Oh the land of cloud - less day! Oh the land of an un - cloud-ed day! Oh they

tell me of a home where no storm-clouds rise, oh they tell me of an un-cloud-ed day. 2. Oh they day.

Additional Lyrics

2. Oh they tell me of a home where my friends have gone,
Oh they tell me of that land far away
Where the tree of life in eternal bloom
Sheds its fragrance through the unclouded day.

3. Oh they tell me of a King in His beauty there,
And they tell me that mine eyes shall behold
Where He sits on the throne that is whiter than snow
In the city that is made of gold.

4. Oh they tell me that He smiles on His children there,
And His smile drives their sorrows all away;
And they tell me that no tears ever come again
In that lovely land of unclouded day.

Wayfaring Stranger

Southern American Folk Hymn

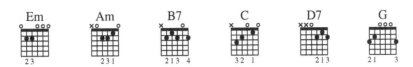

Strum Pattern: 3
Pick Pattern: 4

Additional Lyrics

2. I know dark clouds will gather round me,
   I know my way is rough and steep;
   But golden fields lie out before me
   Where God's redeemed shall ever sleep.
   I'm going there to see my mother
   She said she'd meet me when I come.
   I'm only going over Jordan,
   I'm only going over home.

3. I'll soon be free from ev'ry trial,
   My body sleep in the church yard;
   I'll drop the cross of self denial
   And enter on my great reward.
   I'm going there to see my Savior
   To sing His praise forever more.
   I'm only going over Jordan,
   I'm only going over home.

We Are So Blessed

Words and Music by Greg Nelson, Gloria and William J. Gaither

Additional Lyrics

2. We are so blessed by the things You have done,
   The vict'ries You've won and what You've brought us through.
   We are so blessed, take what we have to bring.
   Take it all ev'rything, Lord, we bring it to You.

We Shall Behold Him

Words and Music by Dottie Rambo

Strum Pattern: 7, 8
Pick Pattern: 8

1. The sky shall un-fold, _____ pre-par-ing His en-trance. _____ The
2. *See additional lyrics*

stars shall ap-plaud _____ Him _____ with thun-ders of praise. _____ The sweet

light in His eyes shall _____ en-hance those _____ a-wait-ing, _____ and

we shall _____ be-hold Him _____ then, face _____ to face. _____

Chorus

We shall _____ be-hold Him, we shall be-hold Him _____

face to face in all of His glo-ry. _____ We shall _____ be-

hold Him, we shall be-hold Him _____

face to face, _____ our Sav - ior _____ and Lord. _____ 2. The

$\oplus$ **Coda**

face to face, _____ our Sav - ior and

Lord. _____ Face to face, _____

_____ our Sav - ior and Lord! _____

Additional Lyrics

2. The angel shall sound the shout of His coming.
   The sleeping shall rise from their slumbering place.
   And those who remain shall be changed in a moment;
   And we shall behold Him then face to face.

Whispering Hope

Words and Music by Alice Hawthorne

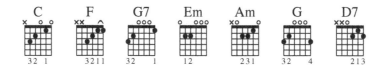

Strum Pattern: 7
Pick Pattern: 7, 9

Verse
Moderately

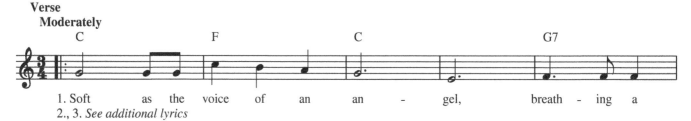

1. Soft as the voice of an an - gel, breath - ing a
2., 3. *See additional lyrics*

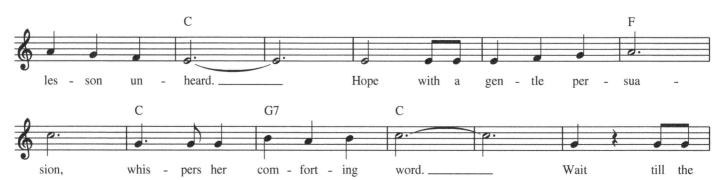

les - son un - heard. _____ Hope with a gen - tle per - sua -

sion, whis - pers her com - fort - ing word. _____ Wait till the

dark - ness is o - ver, wait till the tem - pest is done. _____

Hope for the sun - shine to - mor - row, af - ter the show - er is

Chorus

gone. _____ Whis - per - ing hope. _____ Oh, how

wel - come thy voice. _____ Mak - ing my

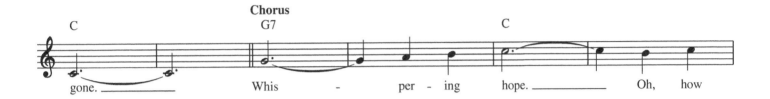

1.

heart _____ in the sor - row re - joice. _____

2.

heart _____ in the sor - row re - joice. _____

Additional Lyrics

2. If, in the dusk of the twilight,
   Dim be the region afar.
   Will not the deepening darkness
   Brighten the glimmering star?
   Then when the night is upon us,
   Why should the heart sink away?
   When the dark midnight is over,
   Watch for the breaking of day.

3. Hope, as an anchor so steadfast,
   Rends the dark veil for the soul,
   Wither the master has entered,
   Robbing the grave of it's soul.
   Come then, oh come, glad fruition,
   Come to my sad weary heart.
   Come, oh thou blest hope of glory,
   Never, oh never depart.

We'll Understand It Better By and By

Words and Music by Charles A. Tindley

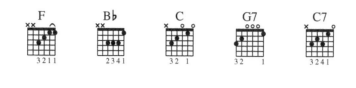

Strum Pattern: 4
Pick Pattern: 3

Verse
Moderately

1. Tri-als dark on ev-'ry hand, and we can-not un-der-stand all the ways that God would lead us to that
2., 3. *See additional lyrics*

bless-ed Prom-ised Land. But He'll guide us with His eye, and we'll fol-low till we die; we will

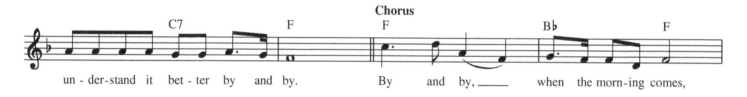

un-der-stand it bet-ter by and by. By and by, ____ when the morn-ing comes,

when the saints of God are gath-ered home, we will tell the sto - ry

how we've o - ver-come; we will un-der-stand it bet-ter by and by. 2. Oft our by.

Additional Lyrics

2. Oft our cherished plans have failed; disappointments have prevailed
   And we've wandered in the darkness, heavy-hearted and alone.
   But we're trusting in the Lord, and according to His Word
   We will understand it better by and by.

3. Temptations, hidden snares often take us unawares
   And our hearts are made to bleed for some thoughtless word or deed;
   And we wonder why the test when we try to do our best
   But we'll understand it better by and by.

Were You There?

Traditional Spiritual
Harmony by Charles Winfred Douglas

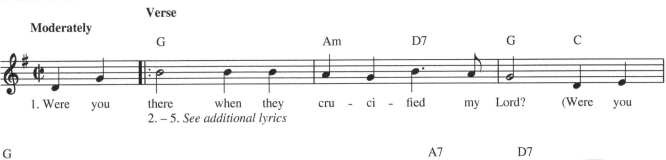

Strum Pattern: 3
Pick Pattern: 3

Verse
Moderately

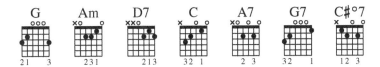

1. Were you there when they cru-ci-fied my Lord? (Were you
2. – 5. *See additional lyrics*

there?) Were you there when they cru-ci-fied my Lord. _____ Oh, _____

some-times it caus-es me to trem-ble, trem-ble, trem-ble. Were you there when they

cru-ci-fied my Lord? (Were you there?) 2. Were you tomb? (In the tomb?)

Additional Lyrics

2. Were you there when they nailed Him to the tree? (To the tree?)
   Were you there when they nailed Him to the tree?
   Oh, sometimes it causes me to tremble, tremble, tremble.
   Were you there when they nailed him to the tree? (To the tree?)

3. Were you there when they pierced Him in the side? (In the side?)
   Were you there when they pierced Him in the side?
   Oh, sometimes it causes me to tremble, tremble, tremble.
   Were you there when they pierced Him in the side? (In the side?)

4. Were you there when the sun refused to shine? (Were you there?)
   Were you there when the sun refused to shine?
   Oh, sometimes it causes me to tremble, tremble, tremble.
   Were you there when the sun refused to shine? (Were you there?)

5. Were you there when they laid Him in the tomb? (In the tomb?)
   Were you there when they laid Him in the tomb?
   Oh, sometimes it causes me to tremble, tremble, tremble.
   Were you there when they laid Him in the tomb? (In the tomb?)

What a Day That Will Be

Words and Music by Jim Hill

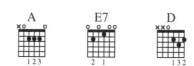

Strum Pattern: 9
Pick Pattern: 9

Verse

Moderately

1. There is com - ing a day when no heart - aches shall come, no more clouds in the sky, no more
2. *See additional lyrics*

tears to dim the eye. All is peace for - ev - er - more on that hap - py gold-en shore, what a

Chorus

day, glo - ri - ous day that will be. _____ What a day that will be when my

Je - sus I shall see, and I look up - on His face, the One who saved me by His

grace. When He takes me by the hand, and leads me through the Prom-ised Land, what a

day, glo - ri - ous day that will be. _____ **1.** 2. There'll be **2.** be. _____

Additional Lyrics

2. There'll be no sorrow there, no more burdens to bear,
No more sickness, no pain, no more parting over there.
And forever I will be with the One who died for me,
What a day, glorious day that will be.

What a Friend We Have in Jesus

Words by Joseph M. Scriven
Music by Charles C. Converse

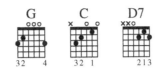

Strum Pattern: 6
Pick Pattern: 4

Verse
Moderately

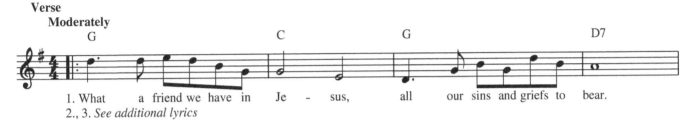

1. What a friend we have in Je - sus, all our sins and griefs to bear.
2., 3. *See additional lyrics*

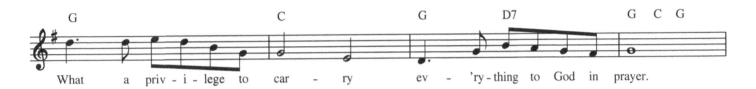

What a priv - i - lege to car - ry ev - 'ry-thing to God in prayer.

Oh, what peace we of - ten for - feit, oh, what need - less pain we bear.

All be-cause we do not car - ry ev - 'ry-thing to God in prayer. there.

Additional Lyrics

2. Have we trials and temptations,
Is there trouble anywhere?
We should never be discouraged;
Take it to the Lord in prayer.
Can we find a friend so faithful
Who will all our sorrows share?
Jesus knows our ev'ry weakness;
Take it to the Lord in prayer.

3. Are we weak and heavy laden,
Cumbered with a load of care?
Precious Savior still our refuge;
Take it to the Lord in prayer.
Do thy friends despise, forsake thee?
Take it to the Lord in prayer.
In His arms He'll take and shield thee;
Thou will find a solace there.

When I Can Read My Title Clear

Words by Isaac Watts
Traditional American Melody attributed to Joseph C. Lowry

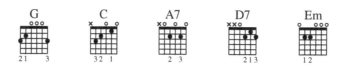

Strum Pattern: 4
Pick Pattern: 4

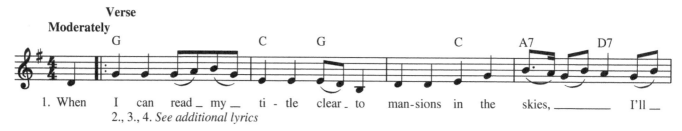

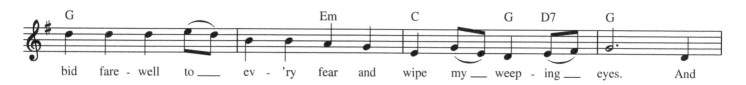

1. When I can read my title clear to man-sions in the skies, I'll
2., 3., 4. *See additional lyrics*

bid fare-well to ev-'ry fear and wipe my weep-ing eyes. And

wipe my weep-ing eyes, and wipe my weep-ing eyes, I'll

bid fare-well to ev-'ry fear and wipe my weep-ing eyes. 2. Should breast.

Additional Lyrics

2. Should earth against my soul engage, and fiery darts be hurled,
   Then I can smile at Satan's rage and face a frowning world.
   And face a frowning world, and face a frowning world,
   Then I can smile at Satan's rage and a face a frowning world.

3. Let cares like a wild deluge come, and storms of sorrow fall!
   May I but safely reach my home, my God, my heav'n, my all.
   My God, my heav'n, my all, my God, my heav'n, my all,
   May I but safely reach my home, my God, my heav'n, my all.

4. There shall I bathe my weary soul in seas of heav'nly rest,
   And not a wave of trouble roll across my peaceful breast.
   Across my peaceful breast, across my peaceful breast.
   And not a wave of trouble roll across my peaceful breast.

When the Roll Is Called Up Yonder

Words and Music by James M. Black

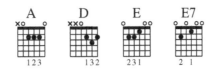

Strum Pattern: 4
Pick Pattern: 6

Verse

Joyfully

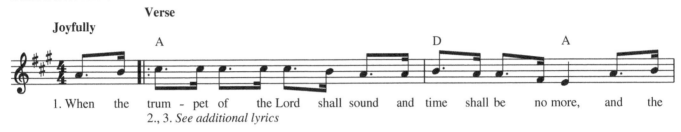

1. When the trum - pet of the Lord shall sound and time shall be no more, and the
2., 3. *See additional lyrics*

morn - ing breaks, e - ter - nal, bright and fair; when the saved of earth shall gath - er o - ver

on the oth - er shore and the roll is called up yon - der, I'll be there! When the

Chorus

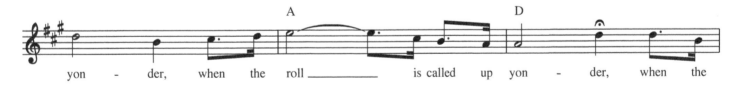

roll _____ is called up yon - der, when the roll _____ is called up

yon - der, when the roll _____ is called up yon - der, when the

roll is called up yon - der, I'll be there! 2. On that there!

Additional Lyrics

2. On that bright and cloudless morning
   When the dead in Christ shall rise,
   And the glory of His resurrection share;
   When His chosen ones shall gather
   To their home beyond the skies
   And the roll is called up yonder, I'll be there!

3. Let us labor for the Master
   From the dawn till setting sun,
   Let us talk of all His wondrous love and care;
   Then when all of life is over
   And our work on earth is done
   And the roll is called up yonder, I'll be there!

When We All Get to Heaven

Words by Eliza E. Hewitt
Music by Emily D. Wilson

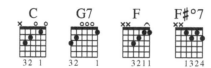

Strum Pattern: 2, 3
Pick Pattern: 3, 4

Verse
Moderately

1. Sing the won-drous love _ of __ Je - sus, sing His mer - cy __ and His grace.
2., 3., 4. *See additional lyrics*

In the man - sions, bright and bless - ed, He'll pre - pare for us a place. When we

Chorus

all get to heav - en, what a day of re-joic - ing that will be! When we

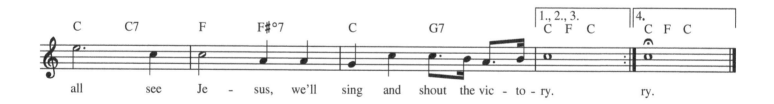

all see Je - sus, we'll sing and shout the vic - to - ry. ry.

Additional Lyrics

2. While we walk the pilgrim pathway,
Clouds will overspread the sky;
But when trav'ling days are over,
Not a shadow, not a sigh!

3. Let us then be true and faithful,
Trusting, serving ev'ryday.
Just one glimpse of Him in glory
Will the toils of life repay.

4. Onward to the prize before us!
Soon His beauty we'll behold.
Soon the pearly gates will open,
We shall tread the streets of gold.

Why Me?

(Why Me, Lord?)

Words and Music by Kris Kristofferson

Strum Pattern: 8
Pick Pattern: 8

Intro
Moderately

Verse

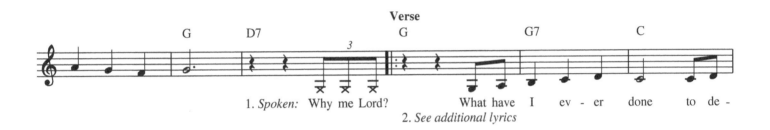

1. *Spoken:* Why me Lord? What have I ev - er done to de -
2. *See additional lyrics*

serve e - ven one of the plea - sures ___ I've known? ___ *Spoken:* Tell me Lord,

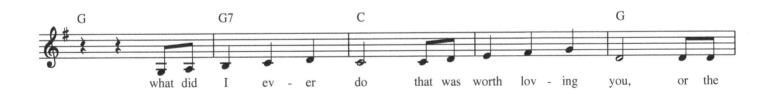

what did I ev - er do that was worth lov - ing you, or the

𝄋 Chorus

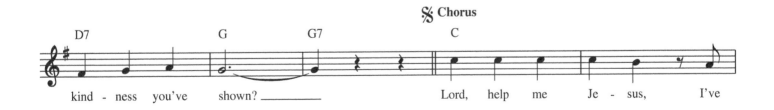

kind - ness you've shown? ___ Lord, help me Je - sus, I've

wast - ed it so, help me Je - sus, I know what I am. ____

But now that I know that I've need - ed you so, help me

To Coda ⊕ 1.   2.   *D.S. al Coda*

Je - sus, my soul's in your hands.   2. *Spoken:* Try me Lord, hands.

⊕ **Coda**

hands. ____   Je - sus, my soul's in your hands. ____

Additional Lyrics

2. Try me, Lord, if you think there's a way
   I can try to repay all I've taken from you.
   Maybe Lord, I can show someone else
   What I've been thru myself, on my way back to you.

Wonderful Grace of Jesus

Words and Music by Haldor Lillenas

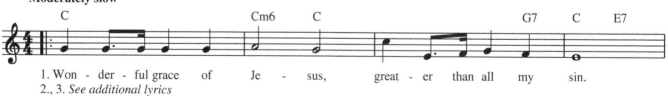

Strum Pattern: 1, 3
Pick Pattern: 2, 4

Verse
   Moderately slow

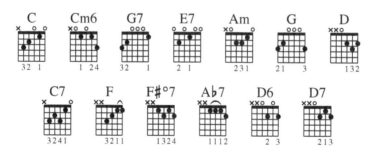

1. Won - der - ful grace of Je - sus, great - er than all my sin.
2., 3. *See additional lyrics*

Additional Lyrics

2. Wonderful grace of Jesus, reaching to all the lost.
By it I have been pardoned, saved to the uttermost.
Chains have been torn asunder, giving me liberty;
For the wonderful grace of Jesus reaches me.

3. Wonderful grace of Jesus, reaching the most defiled.
By its transforming power making Him God's dear child.
Purchasing peace and heaven for all eternity;
For the wonderful grace of Jesus reaches me.

Will the Circle Be Unbroken

Words by Ada R. Habershon
Music by Charles H. Gabriel

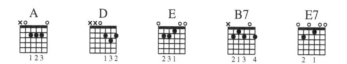

Strum Pattern: 5
Pick Pattern: 5

1. I was stand - ing by my win - dow, on one cold and cloud - y day when I
2., 3. *See additional lyrics*

saw the hearse come roll - ing, for to take my Mo - ther a - way. Will the

Chorus

cir - cle be un - bro - ken, by and by, Lord, by and by? There's a

bet - ter home a - wait - ing, in the sky, in the sky. 2. Oh, I sky.

Additional Lyrics

2. Oh, I told the undertaker, "Undertaker please drive slow,
   For this body you are hauling, Lord, I hate to see her go."

3. I will follow close behind her, try to hold up and be brave;
   But I could not hide my sorrow, when they laid her in her grave.

Wings of a Dove

Words and Music by Bob Ferguson

Strum Pattern: 8
Pick Pattern: 9

Verse

Moderately

1. When trou - bles sur - round us, _____ when e - vils

2., 3. See additional lyrics

come, _____ the bod - y grows weak; _____ the

spir - it grows numb. _____ When these things be - set us, _____ He

does - n't for - get us. _____ He sends down His love _____

on the wings of a dove. _____ On the wings of a

Chorus

snow white dove. He sends His pure sweet

love, a sign from a - bove _____ on the wings of a

1., 2.

dove. _____ 2. When No - ah had

3.

dove. _____

Additional Lyrics

2. When Noah had drifted on the flood many days,
   He searched for land in various ways.
   Troubles he had some but wasn't forgotten.
   He sent him His love on the wings of a dove.

3. When Jesus went down to the waters that day,
   He was baptized in the usual way.
   When it was done, God blessed His Son.
   He sent him his love on the wings of a dove.

Without Him

Words and Music by Mylon R. LeFevre

Strum Pattern: 9
Pick Pattern: 9

Verse

Flowing

1. With-out Him I could do noth-ing, with-out Him I'd sure-ly
2. *See additional lyrics*

fall; with-out Him I would be drift-ing like a

ship with-out a sail.

Chorus

Je-sus, oh Je-sus, do you know Him to-day? You can't turn Him a-

way. Oh, Je-sus, oh Je-sus with-

1. out Him, how lost I would be. 2. With- be.

Additional Lyrics

2. Without Him I would be dying, without Him I'd be enslaved;
Without Him life would be hopeless, but with Jesus, thank God, I'm saved.

The Wonder of It All

Words and Music by George Beverly Shea

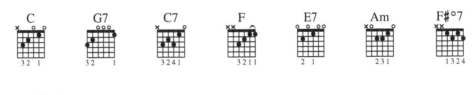

Strum Pattern: 7, 8
Pick Pattern: 7, 8

Warmly

Verse

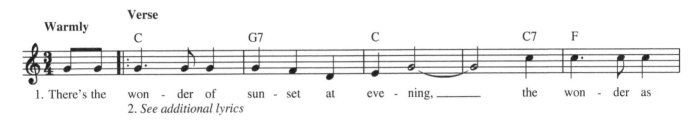

1. There's the won-der of sun-set at eve-ning, _____ the won-der as
2. *See additional lyrics*

sun - rise I see; _____ but the won - der of won - ders that

thrills my _ soul is the won-der that God loves me. _____ Oh, the

Chorus

won - der of it all, the won - der of it all, just to think that

God _ loves me! _____ O, the won - der of it all, the won - der of it

all, just to think that God _ loves me! _____ 2. There's the me! _____

Additional Lyrics

2. There's the wonder of springtime and harvest,
   The sky, the stars, the sun;
   But the wonder of wonders that thrills my soul
   Is a wonder that's only begun.

Written in Red

Words and Music by Gordon Jensen

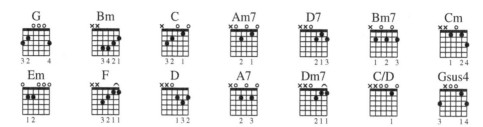

Strum Pattern: 8, 9
Pick Pattern: 8, 9

Verse
Slowly

1. In let - ters ___ of crim - son God wrote His love on a hill - side ___ so
2. *See additional lyrics*

long, long ___ a - go. ___ For you and for me, Je - sus

died and love's great - est sto - ry was told. ___ "I

Chorus

love you, I love you," that's what

Cal - va - ry said. ___ "I love you, I love ___

you, ___ I love you," writ - ten ___ in red. ___ ___

Additional Lyrics

2. Down through the ages God wrote His love
   With the same hands that suffered and bled,
   Giving all He had to give, a message so easily read.